GET
RICH
SLOW

GET
RICH
SLOW

Start NOW.
Start SMALL.
Achieve REAL WEALTH.

SARAH RIEGELHUTH

Wrightbooks

First published in 2013 by Wrightbooks
an imprint of John Wiley & Sons Australia, Ltd
42 McDougall St, Milton Qld 4064

Office also in Melbourne

Typeset in ITC Berkeley Oldstyle Std 11/13

National Library of Australia Cataloguing-in-Publication entry:

Author:	Riegelhuth, Sarah.
Title:	Get rich slow: Start now. Start small. Achieve real wealth. / Sarah Riegelhuth.
ISBN:	9781118406168 (pbk.)
Notes:	Includes index.
Subjects:	Finance, Personal.
Dewey Number:	332.024

Internal design by Peter Reardon, pipelinedesign.com.au

Cover design by Paul McCarthy

Author image © Karen Woo

Printed in China by Printplus Limited

10 9 8 7 6 5 4 3 2 1

Disclaimer
The material in this publication is of the nature of general comment only, and does not represent professional advice. It is not intended to provide specific guidance for particular circumstances and it should not be relied on as the basis for any decision to take action or not take action on any matter which it covers. Readers should obtain professional advice where appropriate, before making any such decision. To the maximum extent permitted by law, the author and publisher disclaim all responsibility and liability to any person, arising directly or indirectly from any person taking or not taking action based on the information in this publication.

*For Finn (my love) and Mark
(my best mate) for both always,
always believing in me.*

Contents

About the author

Sarah Riegelhuth is the co-founder of award-winning financial advisory firm Wealth Enhancers and the highly successful League of Extraordinary Women, an organisation supporting the development of young female entrepreneurs nationally. She is passionately committed to helping women realise their potential, both financially and in all aspects of their lives.

Named as one of Melbourne's Top 100 most influential, inspiring and creative citizens by *The Age* in 2011, Sarah is recognised as one of Australia's leading female entrepreneurs. An accomplished keynote speaker, Sarah is also a popular blogger, writer and columnist for several online and print publications including *Women's Agenda* and *Money Management*.

In 2010, Sarah became the youngest board member in the history of the Association of Financial Advisers (AFA) and helped the association launch the inaugural Female Excellence in Advice Award. The award has been more successful than any other award established by the AFA.

Outside of business and finance, Sarah can be found running along the beach in Melbourne, enjoying snow sports or travelling the world.

Here's how you can connect to Sarah:

Websites:
www.sarahriegelhuth.com.au
www.wealthenhancers.com.au
www.leagueofextraordinarywomen.com.au

Twitter:
@SarahRiegelhuth

@WealthEnhancers
@TheLeagueAust

LinkedIn:
http://au.linkedin.com/in/sarahriegelhuth

Facebook:
www.facebook.com/sarahjaneriegelhuth

Vimeo:
vimeo.com/channels/sarahriegelhuth

Acknowledgements

This book would never have been possible if it weren't for the incredible, amazing and supportive people whom I am lucky to share my life with.

To my one true love, Finn Kelly, for his love, support, proofreading, encouragement and for always believing in me even before I do.

To my Dad, the other man in my life, for giving me the opportunity to work with him, learn from him and for teaching me most of what I know about business and finance.

To my Mum, for teaching me to be a good person and to treat everyone equally.

To my sister, Emma — my best friend — thank you for always being there for me, for writing inspiration and grammar tips!

To Keryn Batsilas and our team at Wealth Enhancers, for their ongoing excitement, enthusiasm and contagious passion for what we do.

To the League girls, Sheryl Thai, Liz Atkinson and Marie Cruz, working with you is unbelievable. I feel blessed to have found you, to have created what we have, and to know such inspirational women.

To all my clients, without you I wouldn't know what I know.

To all of my friends who stick around even though I work too much, and never seem to have any time. You know who you are, thank you, thank you.

To Kristin Ormrod for reviewing the insurance information in chapter 16 and to Danielle Neale for reviewing the parenting section in chapter 12.

Lastly, but importantly, thank you to Lucy Raymond and Wiley for finding me, and for believing in this book.

Preface

For years the idea of writing a book that could inspire others to take control of their finances had played on my mind. I just wasn't sure how to go about it. The way any good idea does, it ticked away in the back of my mind, surfacing from time to time when a new approach or a different angle occurred to me. It still didn't feel right, though, until an inspiring conversation with my best friend, Mark.

We were strolling along Swanston Street in Melbourne, both about to rush off to other engagements—Mark to the football and me to an Unconvention to launch the League of Extraordinary Women. We had been discussing what was, in our opinion, the secret to success, and had decided that it all came down to executing and following through with an idea, rather than the idea itself. Ideas are a dime a dozen. The difference between those who make it and those who just have the good idea is getting out there and *getting it done* ... and not giving up when the going gets tough, which it almost always does at some point or another.

My subconscious must have continued to turn over this conversation because the next afternoon, as I was dozing on the couch, it all came to me in a rush, the way thoughts tumble through your mind suddenly when you're in that half-awake, half-dreaming state. My eyes shot open, I grabbed my iPad and immediately keyed in the book's title and roughly mapped out the chapter titles. 'I've got it!' I announced to my partner, Finn. I was going to write this book, and now I knew how to do it.

And here it is! By sharing what I had learned in 10 years as a financial adviser, along with some of my own personal experiences and those of my clients, I hope to inspire and empower you by equipping you with the tools you need to make positive life changes and take control of your finances. When we take control we let go of excuses, stop waiting for simple solutions or engaging in 'magical thinking', develop an understanding of the psychology of money, and arm ourselves with the information we need to set goals, develop an action plan and follow through.

The approach I have taken in this book is relatively straightforward, I'll admit, yet it goes against the grain of most books about wealth creation available today, which generally focus on getting rich *quickly*. This book suggests that the opposite road is the surer one. The trend towards sustainable and rewarding wealth creation emerged in the wake of the global financial crisis. The key concept here is slow money.

The slow money approach to financial security is all about starting small but starting now, and slowly, surely building long-term, sustainable wealth throughout your life. The main principles of slow money can be summarised like this: (1) spend less than you earn; (2) begin saving and investing today; (3) set lifestyle goals, and link your wealth creation to these goals; (4) segment and track your savings and spending; and (5) evaluate your purchases and insist on value for money. By following these principles, using a little discipline and taking advantage of the power of compound interest, anyone can build wealth sustainably over the long term, and feel good doing it!

Of course, by far the best time to learn and adopt these principles is when we're young, before unwise spending patterns and poor decision making have cast us into a world of debt. That's why this book speaks particularly, although certainly not exclusively, to readers aged in their 20s to 40s. Many will be young professionals with the monetary resources to succeed, but because of their relationship with money, they have found it difficult to break bad habits and get ahead.

For 10 years I've worked with people from all walks of life, ages and income levels and I've seen it all—from the senior medical director earning $400 000 a year retiring with no assets and only $200 000 in super (which would last him six months), to the teacher on a modest wage who managed to retire at 55 with more than $1 million in super (which will last her to the end of her days). The one thing I've learned is that it's really quite simple to build wealth. If you don't overcomplicate it, or persuade yourself you'll never be wealthy because of your wage level, you *can* achieve financial security.

Get Rich Slow cuts right to the chase to help you make the most of your financial situation. The book is organised into three parts, each of which focuses on one of three overarching goals: facing your current financial situation, learning what you need to know about money management and getting started on your own journey to financial security.

This journey begins, as chapter 1 outlines, with taking personal responsibility for your situation. Chapter 2 warns of the false promise of quick money schemes and luck over hard work, determination and a different way of thinking. The next two chapters focus on debt control and the importance of distinguishing between good and bad debt. Finally in this part, chapter 5 argues passionately against deferring change to another day, because time is the one variable we cannot control.

Part II explores the main investment vehicles available to us, reviewing the roles cash (chapter 7), shares (chapter 8) and property (chapter 9) can play in helping us to achieve our financial goals, while also recognising another essential, often overlooked asset — our own earnings potential (chapter 10). The part closes with a review of the greatest savings vehicle of them all — superannuation (chapter 11).

The first two chapters of part III explore the fascinating subject of the psychology of money: when it comes to our attitudes to money and financial decision making, our upbringing, beliefs and habitual patterns of behaviour are surprisingly influential, and we need to understand these influences to avoid limiting our financial outcomes. In chapter 14 we take stock of our resources by completing a budget and financial position assessment. In the next, most important chapter we set our specific financial goals, prioritise them and establish exactly how and by when we will achieve them. We are now well on our way, but, as chapter 16 warns, without the security of adequate insurance cover, all our carefully laid plans are potentially exposed to events beyond our control. None of the steps to financial security I set out in this book need be especially complex or intimidating. Still, as discussed in the final chapter, seeking the advice of a financial adviser, accountant or other expert is highly recommended, as is sharing your journey with friends.

I hope you enjoy this book. I hope you put the lessons shared to good use, and I wish you a lifetime of prosperity.

PART I

Let's
get
real

CHAPTER 1

What are **you** waiting for?

You cannot escape the responsibility of tomorrow by evading it today.

Abraham Lincoln

Someone once wrote, in relation to taking personal financial responsibility, 'A man is not a financial plan'. I can't remember where I first read this, and I've certainly heard it a number of times since, but it rang so true to me I just had to open the book with it. As an independent teenager who worked from the age of 14, I always had money to save for things I wanted and to spend on having fun with friends. Maybe because of this, and because of my parents' separation when I was still young, I never really considered the idea that a man, or even my parents, would be my path to financial security.

So it surprised me to find that many people do consider their personal financial wellbeing to be the responsibility of someone else, whether their own parents, a partner, an employer, the government, or even friends or extended family. Many convince themselves that the financial situation they are in is out of their control and wait for outside factors, things they cannot influence, to change in order for their own position to improve. We all lose our way from time to time, and I have been guilty of falling into this mindset in the past too. The important thing is to recognise the signs and to start to change the way you think.

An ancient lesson

Lao Tzu, the ancient Chinese philosopher and founder of Taoism, sums up the power of our thoughts beautifully:

> *Watch your thoughts; they become words. Watch your words; they become actions. Watch your actions; they become habit. Watch your habits; they become character. Watch your character; it becomes your destiny.*

If we indulge in a belief that our financial situation is not our responsibility, ultimately we will create a reality in which our finances are indeed out of control. It all starts with our thoughts, because over time they will play out in our actions. If we can create positive thoughts, in any area of our life . . . well, you can imagine what will start to happen.

Common mindset traps

In my professional role as a financial adviser, I am often taken by surprise when seemingly confident and successful professional women—highly educated executives who lead teams, run corporations and make tough decisions—come to see me with two budgets prepared. The first is their actual budget; the second includes the income of a fictional 'Prince Charming' who is waiting 'just around the corner' to sweep them off their feet and provide for them. They actually spend precious time factoring this into their financial plan.

I've also come across men who run apparently successful businesses but are up to their eyeballs in debt—for which they blame the tax office, their suppliers, their clients, their professional advisers and whoever else they can think of, rather than the simple fact that they've mismanaged their money and have been living beyond their means. I commonly hear business owners blaming their accountants for not making them aware of their tax liabilities, when the reality is they simply *spent* everything in the bank account and didn't set anything aside for the tax that always must be paid. It's pretty simple: if you earn money (which is a good thing), you'll have to pay some tax (not so great, but unavoidable).

I've seen young couples with small children argue that they don't really need any insurance or savings, because their parents will help them out if they ever get into difficulties. I've even seen people completely unphased by mounting credit card debt . . . because they have a ticket in next week's lottery!

There's nothing wrong with dreaming a little. I've no problem with this—in fact I do it too, we all do. If we seriously want to create financial security for ourselves, though, it has to start with us. Right now. No-one else can do it for us. Waiting on, relying on or blaming other people will get us nowhere in a hurry. The first hard truth we need to swallow is that whatever financial situation we are in is completely, 100 per cent, of our own making. Whether it's good, bad or ugly, we created it. No more excuses.

But this is not just about the negative situations. It's important too to pat ourselves on the back if and when we do well financially. This is generally a result of hard work and discipline and is nothing to be shy about. Despite how it might appear on the outside, those who are successful have in most cases worked very hard for that success.

Have a go at this quiz to get an idea of how financially responsible you really are.

Quiz: Are you financially responsible?

1 You moved house a few months ago and have just received a call from the bank to say they've put your credit card on hold, because you haven't made a payment for over 90 days. You face a late fee and additional interest charges. Do you:

(a) blame the bank for not tracking you down after the move?

(b) become really frustrated with yourself for forgetting to make the payment, but also with the bank for not contacting you sooner?

(c) know that this wouldn't happen to you, because you have a direct debit set-up and you pay off your card in full each month?

2   You've been working for the same employer for some time and think you deserve a pay rise. Do you:

   (a) complain to your teammates about how tight the company is?

   (b) work harder for the next six months, hoping someone will notice?

   (c) point out to your boss that you addressed this issue at your last employee review, showing your boss the additional work you were doing and proving your worth?

3   Your best friend suggests the two of you go on a trip to Las Vegas. The trip is planned for six months' time. Do you:

   (a) decide not to worry about financing it? (You'll put the whole thing on your credit card and deal with the bills later.)

   (b) agree to go, even though you're not sure how you're going to pay for it? (You'll save a little between now and then, and fund the additional expenses on your credit card.)

   (c) calculate that it will fit into your annual holiday budget, for which you put a little away each week? (So you agree enthusiastically.)

4   You read an article in the weekend paper about superannuation and the fact that many Australians don't have anywhere near enough money to last them through their retirement. Do you:

   (a) not even bother to finish reading it? (You have about five super funds floating around. You don't know anything about super but figure the government will look after you through the age pension.)

   (b) not give it very much thought? (You consolidated all your super funds a while ago. You've considered adding to your fund, but you're not really sure how super works anyway, so you'll worry about it more when you get older.)

   (c) read it with peace of mind? (You have one super fund and have been salary sacrificing a little into your fund each pay cycle since you started full-time work. It's a long-term savings plan, which you understand is easier to get started on early.)

5 The interest rate on your mortgage has increased a couple of times and it's getting harder to afford the repayments. Do you:

(a) blame the bank for lending you so much? How did they expect you to cope with these rate rises, especially when you have no savings in the bank?

(b) tough it out, using your credit card when you need to? You knew you probably shouldn't have borrowed this much but had hoped that the rates wouldn't increase as they have.

(c) feel disappointed by the interest rate rise, while knowing you were prepared for this and didn't borrow more than you could confidently afford to repay? You've got a savings buffer account and have been making extra loan repayments, so it shouldn't trouble you too much.

How did you score?

Mostly As: Sounds like you've been spending most of your time blaming everyone else for your unhealthy bank balance. It's time to get on top of it and recognise that it starts with you, and it starts *now*. You need to start taking responsibility for every financial decision you make, considering the long-term effects as well as the short-term benefits. Part I of this book is going to be really important for you, but don't stop there. You'll need to read parts II and III to learn the skills required to create a financial plan and follow through with it.

Mostly Bs: You've started to realise that you need to take control of your financial situation. It sounds as though you've begun that journey, so great work. Making a start is better than not starting at all. Remember always to plan for the future and forgive yourself for the mistakes of the past. You'll like part II of this book in particular as it'll help you build your knowledge further, and part III will give you the motivation to keep up the good work.

Mostly Cs: You're on track and taking full responsibility for your financial situation. Keep learning about money, by reading books like this (especially the educational chapters in part II), and remember to reward yourself for your hard work and discipline.

Accepting responsibility

Are you waiting on someone or something else to change your life? The first step towards achieving success in any area of your life is to accept that you are wholly and solely responsible for your future. Sure, life will always throw you a curve-ball, be it positive or negative, but your response, the next step you take, is still solely your choice.

I want to share with you a particular lesson I learned that changed my life in a huge way. Like all of life's teachings, it wasn't an easy lesson to learn, but it was well worth the tough time as I believe it helped shape me into who I am today.

My wake-up call

At the age of 19, I returned to Brisbane from a six-month stint in the UK, where I'd worked as a bartender for a few months, saved a little, travelled Europe and came back with a modest credit card debt that felt huge at the time (more on this later). After working three jobs for several months I managed to repay the entire credit card debt and even save enough money to move back to Melbourne, where I planned to begin studying IT.

In the meantime I'd started seeing someone, who told me he was also moving to Melbourne at the end of the year. 'What a coincidence!' I thought at the time. I wasn't looking for anything serious, but before I knew it we were moving in together, using *my* credit card to pay for many of the 'joint' costs associated with moving, using *my* savings for the bond, which was in *his* name . . . well, you start to get the picture. From very early on he had started racking up a debt to me. I soon became uncomfortable with the relationship, but I kept thinking I needed to hang in there in order to recover the money.

I had convinced myself to wait it out until the lease on the apartment was up, otherwise I'd likely lose the bond money as well. The relationship continued to deteriorate while, not surprisingly, the debt escalated. I felt my life was not my own, but I still thought I couldn't leave him because I needed to get my money back. I was staring down the barrel of three years of study and could barely afford my own living costs, let alone the huge credit card debt he had accumulated in my name. How would I pay it off? It seemed an impossible situation and was having an effect on my self-confidence.

I thank my lucky stars I came to my senses after only a few months in Melbourne. Following a long discussion with my friend Mark (who cared more about my mental health than my financial situation), it was clear to me what I needed to do. I recognised that the debt wouldn't be repaid but would simply get bigger, and that I was the only person who could change the situation. I needed to cut my losses, pack my things and get out. Even though this left me with a personal debt of about $4000, I could at least start to repay it without the fear of it accumulating further. I was also much happier being out of the toxic relationship. I was taking baby steps in the right direction, and they were steps of my choosing.

Life lessons

This lesson was about so much more than money. It taught me that whatever I wanted in life was within my reach; it was just up to me, and only me, to take the action required to work towards it. Sometimes making the tough decisions brings a lot of pain. Ultimately, though, when armed with self-belief and the recognition that it is all up to you yourself, anything is possible.

The added benefit of going through something like this is that we learn something that can be applied later in life. Every time we experience a challenge, we come out stronger than before, and it's this strength that can help us avoid making the same mistakes twice.

Many years later I was able to draw on that early experience to make a tough decision to exit a business I had spent much time and energy building. I had contributed a substantial amount of money on a hand-shake agreement (yes, I should have known better!) but discovered, when the paperwork finally arrived, that the partnership deal wasn't legally sound. Lengthy meetings ensued and more empty promises were made, but my gut was telling me what I needed to do. Once again it was time to cut my losses and walk away. Although I lost money, I would have lost much more had I stayed on. If the deal's not right, it's not right — but that's a whole other story!

Being financially independent

Taking responsibility for your own situation is the first step towards achieving financial success. We all need to stop waiting for that man, woman, parent, pay rise or winning lottery ticket and recognise that the power to make positive changes in our own financial situation lies within ourselves alone.

Once we have established this, and begun our personal wealth creation journey, it's crucial that we maintain this sense of personal responsibility and independence, even if we do happen to meet that perfect person. (How many stories do we hear of women or men who have given up their careers to stay at home and look after their children, only for the relationship to break down years later, and for the homemaker to be left with little in terms of wealth and employable skills?) If this is a decision you are thinking of making, it's important you have a candid conversation with your partner about the impact this could have on your finances and employability. Perhaps you can together come up with a plan to ensure the person who stays at home remains a valuable contributor to the financial security of the family.

Case study: Jacinta's story

A client of mine married young, finished university but never joined the workforce. Her traditionalist husband wanted them to have children and for her to stay at home and be a full-time parent, and although this wasn't what she had always dreamed of, she agreed. Her husband ran a successful business and they were very comfortable financially, so at the time the decision made sense.

For several years they lived a comfortable life and she stayed at home and looked after their daughter. In the end he left her. Ironically, one of his reasons was he felt she failed to appreciate money and was too frivolous with her spending. She was left with very little in the way of savings and her credit cards were all cancelled. She knew she would struggle to find employment as she had only ever worked in part-time jobs while studying, not to mention the fact that she had a four-year-old to take care of.

I love this story because it has a great ending. Jacinta took full responsibility for her situation. She knew that if she didn't act quickly she'd be in serious financial trouble. The one thing she was confident she could do well was home cleaning—she had always struggled to find good cleaners. So she got out there and started cleaning houses, better than any of her cleaners ever had. She advertised in the local paper and before she knew it was fully booked and started to make okay money. Over time she hired more cleaners and the business grew. Two years on the business, providing both residential and commercial services, is very successful. Jacinta herself does little cleaning now.

Despite this impressive outcome, it had been very hard for her at the beginning, when she was still dealing with the emotional impact of her marriage breakup and the legal side of it all, as well as looking after her young daughter.

This sink-or-swim scenario had a positive conclusion. Not all of them do, and even Jacinta will admit that had she put aside some money earlier, or built up her skills a little, she certainly wouldn't have been as stressed out during those initial stages. She'd always had it in her to start and run a successful business; she just hadn't thought she needed to worry about it.

Moving forward

Ask yourself right now, what if you never meet your perfect partner or win first prize in the lottery? Is your current life enough? Are you making the right choices so you will always be able to support yourself financially and hold your head high independently? If the answer is no or you're not sure, then it could be time to make some changes.

Do you have a list of excuses as to why you are not in the financial position you'd like to be in? Well, I'm here to tell you right now that no-one's buying it except you, and all you are doing is letting yourself down. By allowing yourself to believe that outside factors are to blame, you are kidding no-one and simply limiting the possibilities that lay ahead. It's not going to be easy. You are going to have to change things; you'll probably even have to go through a period of sacrifice.

But it's almost never as bad as you think, and the outcome of taking full responsibility for your own finances and starting to take your own baby steps towards securing your financial future will be truly rewarding. And this decision will flow into all other areas of your life. You'll become more self-reliant, you'll achieve things you perhaps never thought possible and you'll also be able to help others too. I'm not saying you shouldn't collaborate with others or seek help, or even pursue a relationship in which you share money. That's not it at all.

The simplest analogy I can give is the oxygen mask on the plane scenario. The pre-flight demonstration and instructions are clear: put on your own oxygen mask first, secure it and ensure it is working *before* helping anyone else. Why? Easy: if you're not breathing, you're no use to anyone else. Sort out your own finances, put a plan in place, rely on yourself and other rewards will follow. You may then even be in a position to help others achieve their own financial freedom, and whatever curve-balls life may throw at you, you'll be ready to catch them.

If you still feel as though this is beyond your reach, or you feel overwhelmed, just keep reading. Remember, you have already taken the first step simply by picking up this book. Chapter 2 introduces the principles behind the get rich slow strategy.

Key points

→ Your financial success is no-one else's priority or responsibility.

→ No more excuses. Financial security starts with you taking responsibility and taking action—*now*.

→ Being financially responsible will positively affect other areas of your life.

Putting it into action

We have discussed the importance of positive thinking. Remember that your thoughts will ultimately become your reality. The following exercise will help you to develop positive thinking. Create a list of all of the excuses you've been using for why you're not in the financial position you could be. Now cross out each excuse, think again and write beside it a positive step forward. In table 1.1 I have provided a few examples.

Table 1.1: thinking positively

Current excuse	Positive step forward
~~I don't earn as much as I need to live.~~	I'm lucky to have this job and this opportunity. I'm going to live within my means and maximise the income I earn. I will work hard, and beyond the scope of my role, to demonstrate that I deserve a pay rise.
~~I'll just buy this now, even though I can't afford it. I'll make up for it later.~~	I will start saving now for things I want, instead of buying them before I can afford to. This will mean I'll always have enough. I need to act on this resolution now, not later.
~~I don't care about the interest on my credit card. I'll pay it back later.~~	Paying interest on my credit card is a complete waste of money — money I could be using to save for a holiday or for something else I want. I'm committed to repaying my debt and not paying credit card interest again.
~~Parking inspectors are out to get me. I'm always getting fines.~~	I will always park in authorised places and pay for a ticket. Parking fines are a complete waste of money that could be going towards repaying debt, savings or even a night out.

CHAPTER 2

Get
rich
slow

Slow and steady wins the race.

Aesop

Many of us look for a quick fix or an easy answer to our money troubles. We're convinced that if the stars align and everything goes according to plan, our fiscal problems will soon be solved. There are two fundamental flaws in this strategy. The first is the high odds against such a stellar alignment; the second is that if this windfall were to occur, the chances are we wouldn't use it for what we so desperately wish to use it for now anyway. Sound ridiculous? Yet I have seen it time and time again. The reality is that, if we haven't worked for something, we rarely appreciate the true value of it.

Striking gold?

Let's focus on the first point for now. We often hear stories of people who apparently got lucky with an idea or venture and struck gold. The reality is almost always very different. The business world provides so many great case studies that offer microcosms of life and economic lessons. Here are a couple of examples.

Case study: Facebook — overnight success?

Facebook appears to represent a sensational story in which one young person came up with an original idea and became rich overnight. Don't get me wrong, it truly is an amazing success story, and much more so than most of us could ever hope to match, but Mark Zuckerberg did not in fact become rich 'overnight'. He had a couple of ideas and one of them really took off. He then worked hard for several years, moved his life to California (and convinced others to follow him there), where he continued to build and develop a business that initially didn't make a cent.

Almost immediately following the launch, a lawsuit was filed against him. This would certainly have stopped many of us in our tracks, but Zuckerberg wasn't fazed. With a ridiculous amount of self-belief, he worked on for several years before Facebook really became monetised. Although he received his first venture capital investment six months after he started coding, it wasn't until two and half years later that Microsoft purchased a 1.6 per cent share in the company, instantly turning Zuckerberg into the 'overnight millionaire' we know him as today.

The rest is history. Of course he is now very wealthy, but two years of really hard work with no financial reward is not how most people imagine overnight success.

There are a myriad similar examples out there, but one in particular stands out for me personally.

Case study: Locomote — hard work and focus

Friends of mine own a web development business, Locomote. The company has grown quickly and is now successful and becoming quite well known. They often have people say to them, 'Wow, you guys are an overnight success!' Over lunch, one of the co-founders shared with me the real story, warts and all.

While they were in high school, cousins Ross and David started doing small graphic design jobs to earn some extra pocket money. They continued to work together like this through university, and eventually decided that they wanted to build the little business they had started into something that could sustain them both, something that would grow. After graduation Ross took up a full-time position in IT while David worked on their business, with Ross pitching in after hours and on weekends. After some time, and with a good chance of outside funding coming through, the business started to pick up and Ross quit his job to join David full time. Not long after, the promised investment fell through and the cousins were left with insufficient income to sustain them both.

Frustrated in their aim to expand the design company, they came up with the idea to invest in a bar with some friends, in the hope that it would provide them with a source of passive income so they could continue to focus on the graphic design business. They couldn't have been more wrong. They found they had to put more and more time, energy and money into the bar, which took their focus away from the design firm.

Wisely, they accepted the situation and made the bold decision to cut their losses and sell the bar. At this stage, they knew something had to give. If they were going to build the graphic design business into what they had always dreamed of, they needed to knuckle down and focus.

Then they made another bold decision. They accepted funding from an established entrepreneur who believed in their vision, and as luck would have it that was exactly what they needed to take the business to a new level. They landed a couple of decent contracts and very quickly things improved, putting them on the radar as an 'overnight success story'. It just took quite a few years to get there! Their real story was not exactly what their admirers would have had in mind when complimenting them on their 'instant' success, though.

Luck plays no part

The moral of these stories is clear: 99 per cent of the time, those who seem to have come into wealth overnight have in fact worked long and hard and maintained a very clear focus before reaping the rewards that become visible to others.

As already mentioned, I use business analogies in this book because they illustrate the principles so well, but these principles apply equally well to individuals. It could be suggested that an anaesthetist is lucky because she need work only a 30-hour week to earn an income of $300000 a year. I would argue that luck plays no part in it.

First, she must work hard in high school in order to achieve the grades to be accepted into medicine at university. She then embarks on five or six years of difficult and intensive study. Provided everything goes to plan and she passes all her subjects, her successful completion of the undergraduate medical degree will be followed by a year as a hospital intern. During this year trainee doctors work on average 12-plus hours a day. Her next step is to become a resident, and at some stage down the track, if she is eventually accepted into the anaesthetist program, she will sign up for another five years of study and ridiculously long working hours. Then one day, after all that time, dedication and very hard work, she will ultimately qualify for that large salary and the opportunity to work a little less. Lucky? No. Deserving? Yes.

The other thing for us to consider is that even though our anaesthetist may now be working shorter hours and be paid handsomely for what she does, the responsibility she carries on the job is far greater than most of us will face. Every day someone's life is essentially in her hands.

In the world of personal finance, it is true that every so often someone will get lucky with shares or a property (or some other form of investment) and strike it rich, or at least quickly turn something small into something big. These are the stories we most often hear about because they are the juiciest and most exciting. They can leave us feeling like maybe it's possible for us too; on the other hand, they can make us feel jealous and resentful that life is so easy for someone else but never seems so for us.

But let's break it down a little further. The likelihood of someone who has never invested before, and has never even saved any money before, finding themselves in a situation where they dare to invest a month's salary in a really cheap speculative mining share, only for the company to strike gold the following week, sending the share price soaring and turning our first-time investor into an instant millionaire . . . is, well, rather low.

In reality, the first thing most of us invest in is cash in the bank. We start saving our money in a high-interest online savings account and, commonly enough in Australia, we then one day purchase our first property. It's often not until we have made serious headway on repaying our mortgage that we may consider building an investment portfolio. Even then it will often begin with dipping our toe in the water to purchase shares in large, well-known Australian companies, not the kind of investment portfolio that will turn you into a millionaire overnight.

Eventually one day when we feel we have a large enough share portfolio and own our own home, we might start feeling courageous enough to invest in something wild, something risky, something that we could lose all of our money in but could also produce a much larger return. And then maybe, if we are lucky, have sought quality advice and invested on the right day, at the right prices, just maybe we could strike it rich. Still, it is a bit of a journey, don't you think?

Case study: Dig a little deeper — Ben's investment property

In recent years we have often heard those stories about someone who bought a property for, say, $350 000 and sold it a year later for $450 000. On the surface, stories like this sound really great. You can't argue with a $100 000 profit achieved in 12 months. Or can you?

If we dig a little deeper we'll often find the situation is not quite as clear as it first sounds. In reality, once stamp duty, interest and property improvement costs are taken into account, plus any capital gains tax payable on sale, the actual net profit is often not nearly as great as it originally appeared. One of my clients, Ben, experienced this firsthand when he bought an investment property a couple of years ago, renovated it and sold it just over a year later.

Ben bought a two-bedroom, two-bathroom apartment in the leafy suburb of Kensington in Melbourne's inner north-west for $365 000. He repainted, replaced the carpets and renovated the kitchen and bathrooms for a total cost of $55 000 and sold the property some 16 months later for $497 000. At first glance, it looked as though Ben had made a profit of $77 000, which would have been a great result after not much more than a year, even though he had given up almost every weekend during the period. Once we performed some further analysis (as outlined in table 2.1, overleaf), taking into account other costs associated with the renovation, the stamp duty and the interest payable on the mortgage, his net profit fell to just $22 000—substantially less than what Ben first thought. Although he still came out ahead, considering the time, effort and energy he had put into the renovations, he wasn't convinced he'd do it again in a hurry.

Table 2.1: Ben's costs and profit—a full breakdown

Cost	$	Based on
Purchase price and mortgage	$365 000	100% mortgage secured against another property
Stamp duty	$14 620	Victorian stamp duty rates
Other fees	$2 000	mortgage establishment fee and legal fees
Painting	$3 750	
Carpets	$7 550	
Kitchen	$17 900	
Bathrooms	$26 700	
Miscellaneous	$5 365	
Cost base	**$426 265**	**purchase price + other fees + renovation**
Sale price	**$497 000**	
Assessable capital gain	$70 735	
Capital gains tax payable	$11 141	
Interest expenses	$30 611	6.29% for 16 months
Tax deduction	$9 643	on interest based on 31.5% MTR
Total spent	$119 637	
Total less: tax deduction	$109 995	
Net profit for Ben	**$22 005**	**sale price − purchase price − total spent**

This case study shows how important it is to take into account *all* the relevant costs when weighing up the profitability of any investment, whether it's a business, shares or property. You should also consider including a value on your time if the investment you've made is labour intensive, as Ben's was.

The main point is you need *all* the information before you can make a judgement on wealth creation ventures. History shows us that most people create wealth through hard work, perseverance, quality advice and sticking to a plan. In essence, they get rich slowly.

The formula that will work

The most exciting thing about the get rich slow concept is that you don't need to take risks—you simply need to start working towards your plan slowly and surely. Eventually, over time, your wealth will build and, most important, you will never go backwards again. Why? Because by taking small steps each day towards building wealth, you create good habits that help you to build your own sustainable future. Little by little, day by day, increment by increment, your wealth will increase.

Getting rich slowly may not sound as exciting as life in the fast lane, but the reality is that one method always works and the other most often doesn't! Time is the one thing we simply cannot beat. It is the magic ingredient that will help us create sustainable wealth over the longer term.

It's often said of Gen Y that they want everything now, that they don't want to wait or to put in the hard work required to achieve something. They want to take shortcuts and skip right to the satisfaction, missing the journey. To some degree I have to agree with this, and I'm not ashamed. There is nothing really wrong with wanting everything now. In fact, I think striving for bigger, better and more in life can be a really positive trait. It is important, however, to understand the difference between what we want and what is achievable in the real world. It's also important to learn to enjoy the journey and embrace delayed gratification. It's not only Gen Y who are trying to get rich quickly, though. The desire to beat the odds has always been around and probably always will be.

The slow money rule: if it sounds too good to be true, it probably is.

If you remember this when making any kind of decision, particularly in relation to investment, you will always err on the side of caution. For now, just start thinking about the tortoise and the hare. The slow and steady tortoise won the race because he set himself a plan (to reach the finish line) and slowly but surely worked towards it, while the overconfident hare went to sleep at the wheel! Even if it feels at times as though you're just plodding along, and you really want to get there faster, just remind yourself that, like the tortoise, you are plodding *in the right direction*.

We've been doing it all wrong!

I believe there is a fundamental flaw in the most popular wealth-building strategy in Australia. As mentioned earlier in the chapter, many of us save a little cash in the bank and fairly quickly rush into purchasing a property. Things got very bad before the global financial crisis (GFC) in 2008, when banks started lending buyers up to 100 per cent of a property's purchase price. This meant many people were entering into mortgages with no proven savings ability.

A mortgage is generally a 25- or 30-year commitment attached to the biggest purchase most of us will ever make. Pre-GFC countless people signed up for mortgages without so much as a few thousand dollars in their bank account. 'Rent money is dead money' was the catchphrase of the moment, and no-one wanted to be the last sucker paying rent when they could easily get approval for a 100 per cent loan and purchase a property of their own.

We have since learned some hard lessons. Interest rates went up, followed by widespread redundancies. Interest rates then came back down again but property prices have also fallen substantially since the peak of the market in the 2010. All this aside, it has never really been a good idea to purchase a property before we've proven to ourselves that we can save over the long term and can comfortably meet our ongoing financial commitments.

Many people also borrowed large sums of money to invest in shares during this period, before the sharemarket dropped by approximately half its value, leaving those with loans secured against their shares high and dry. The main reason people were borrowing to invest like this was to gain tax deductions on the interest payable on the loan, but we should never invest purely for the purpose of gaining a tax deduction. Investment decisions should be based on a careful assessment of the proposed investment and the return it can be expected to produce.

So many things were going wrong during these years, but a lot of the behaviours were fuelled by the deep-seated Australian belief that we must own property. Our culture puts such pressure on young people to buy their first property that it can often be viewed as a defining factor in whether someone can be deemed 'successful', or even responsible.

Property can certainly be a great investment, and it plays an important part in most people's wealth creation strategies, but we might find we could achieve far better results if we were to flip the common investment cycle on its head. If we consider the barriers to entry for the three main investment types (as summarised in table 2.2), we can start to understand a clearer pathway to building wealth.

Table 2.2: barriers to entry for the three main investment vehicles

Investment	Barriers to entry
Cash	Very low — less than $1
Shares	Low — as little as a few hundred dollars
Property	High — will usually require borrowed funds

Given that property has the highest barrier to entry, does it really make sense that in Australia it is often the first thing a young person attempts to invest in? Here's a much more sustainable model: following the order of the table above, we begin by investing a little in cash; we build up our savings for some time, then start contributing regularly to a share portfolio; eventually, once we have established ourselves financially, we purchase a property, confident that we can comfortably meet our mortgage commitments.

We'll return to this idea in part II when we delve further into how different investments work, but for now I simply want to open your mind to the possibility of a different way of looking at investment, and a different way of thinking. Meanwhile, in the next chapter we'll look more closely at the debt spiral and how we might set about controlling and overcoming our personal debt.

Key points

→ What looks like overnight success usually isn't.

→ If it sounds too good to be true, it probably is.

→ Hard work, determination and persistence, not luck, offer you the best chance of success in any enterprise.

→ Start thinking differently about the best ways to build your wealth.

Putting it into action

In this chapter we have discussed the concept that slow and steady will win the race. Think about a time in your life when you really wanted something badly and ultimately succeeded in achieving it. It has to be something that wasn't easy for you, but you worked really hard, put all the steps in place and in the end achieved your goal. Everyone has experienced a situation like this at some stage.

Write a paragraph describing how it felt once you had achieved your goal, and how worthwhile it was knowing you had worked very hard to achieve what you really wanted. This is your *inspiration statement*. Stick your *inspiration statement* on your fridge door or mirror or in the front of your diary — somewhere where you'll see it every day. This will be the statement that motivates you to stick to your plan and keep going even when it feels like things aren't happening fast enough.

CHAPTER 3
Aiming
for
'nothing'?

If you aim at nothing, you will hit it every time.

Zig Ziglar

Over the years I have worked as a financial adviser, I have come across many young people with accumulated personal debt, usually attached to credit cards, store cards, personal loans or car loans. In most cases it began with the first credit card they obtained at the age of 18 or 19, when they'd just finished high school and entered the adult world. Often the credit card had a small limit of perhaps $1000 or $2000, which could be exceeded pretty quickly when the feeling of easy money became familiar. Once the credit card approached its limit, a letter from the bank would quickly arrive offering an increase on the card's credit limit. Sometimes these increases were even issued automatically, if you didn't opt out. Perhaps they then applied for another credit card because the first one was completely maxed, or they received a mass mail offering from another financial institution with a deal too good to refuse. A store card slides in there too (hey, no big deal, it's only a $1500 limit), and the spiral has really started.

Things now feel bit stressful, so the next step is often to begin a debt consolidation strategy. A well-meaning banker arranges a personal loan of $6000 to wrap up all of those credit cards and store cards into one easy payment system. Sounds like a great solution: you can repay the whole debt once and for all and then, while your motivation levels are high, you cancel all your credit cards, except perhaps one, just for emergencies of course, with a limit of only $2000 . . . and so the cycle begins again.

The debt spiral

If this is something that has happened to you, you are not alone. I've seen it time and again, and I've also seen many people eventually climb out of the situation and start creating wealth for themselves, and it doesn't even take as long as you'd think, so don't despair!

Your age favours the bank

What a great strategy this is for the banks and lending institutions! They provide small amounts of easy credit at very high rates of interest and then entice consumers into consolidating the accumulated debts into a small loan with a slightly lower rate of interest, which will amount to a lot over the term of the loan, as they have now locked in this rate of interest for five or so years. Not to mention the fact that in all likelihood we'll begin racking up more high-interest easy credit the moment we've signed the loan docs and tidied up round one.

There is absolutely no point blaming the banks for this situation, however, as that won't get us anywhere. No matter how unethical or underhand it may seem, for them it is purely commercial. Banks are (usually) publicly listed companies with many, many shareholders so their first priority is to generate a profit. A young person represents a great opportunity for them, as their income will generally increase over time and the lender has many years to recoup all of the money they have lent, all the while collecting hefty interest payments.

Dreaming of zero

In this situation we may expend a lot of mental energy dreaming of having no debt. Not only dreaming, but also putting payment plans in place and working out, based on our current salary, how much we need to set aside to repay our debt each week or each month. Every so often we manage to reduce the balance owing a little on one credit card, or even to pay something off, only for an unexpected expense to force us to use that credit card again.

In a nutshell, when we are in this cycle, what we are dreaming about or aiming for is actually nothing or, in dollar terms, zero. The most desirable financial balance for someone with accumulated personal debt is commonly $0. It's a little bit sad when you look at it like that, isn't it? Certainly not something anyone would logically aspire to. But when we're carrying around a load of credit card or personal debt, we long for that elusive zero.

Does this sound familiar? It has certainly been a common theme among many of the young people I have dealt with in my career. Our level of debt may remain fairly stable over many years, or increase only slightly each year, after initially accumulating very quickly. Many of us grow 'comfortable' with this level of debt, which sticks within a consistent range. This comfort level is probably determined in part by our friends, family or other influences, but it's a level that feels manageable to us. However, I have also seen it blow out dramatically over time.

The worst thing about this situation is actually not that we have accumulated $5000, $10 000 or even $60 000 in personal debt, but that carrying the debt completely blocks us from building up any wealth at all.

I've seen people carry around $6000 worth of credit card debt, like a heavy suitcase, for more than 10 years. Commonly their debt burden is not really getting any worse; it's just being lugged around as though it is a physical part of them. We live in a society in which we find this situation acutely embarrassing, and we find it really difficult to discuss our spending habits and debt openly. This often leads to a feeling that our debt is a major, insurmountable obstacle; we feel overwhelmed and bear the burden alone, sharing it with no-one.

Counting the cost

Many of us in this situation retreat into a state of denial: we avoid looking at our bills and statements because we don't want to know the extent of our problem and choose to defer thinking about it until we feel we can resolve it. The problem with this response is that we thereby ignore a crucial factor that could best motivate us to break out of the debt cycle — that is, an understanding of what it is really costing us to maintain this level of debt.

Between the annual fees and high interest rates associated with credit cards, the cost of carrying that debt is often very high. Table 3.1 shows just how much credit card debt could be costing you, depending on your level of debt. These figures are based on just one credit card with an interest rate of 18 per cent and an annual fee of $99. Costs could vary quite a bit depending on how many credit cards you have and on interest rate variations.

Table 3.1: the real cost of credit card debt—an example

Card balance	$1000	$2000	$5000	$10000	$15000	$20000	$40000	$60000
Annual interest	$180	$360	$900	$1800	$2700	$3600	$7200	$10800
Annual fee	$99	$99	$99	$99	$99	$99	$99	$99
Total cost	$279	$459	$999	$1899	$2799	$3699	$7299	$10899
Monthly cost	$23	$38	$83	$158	$233	$308	$608	$908
Weekly cost	$5	$9	$19	$37	$54	$71	$140	$210

In this example, I have broken down the annual cost to a monthly and weekly cost to illustrate how much of our income is being used to maintain personal debt. Of course, this cost doesn't reduce the debt at all—it simply covers the cost of maintaining it.

Exercise: What is it costing you?

Collect together your most recent credit card and loan statements. (If you don't receive them in the mail, they will be available online.) Use table 3.2 to work out what it is actually costing you each year if you don't reduce your level of debt.

Table 3.2: calculating your credit card costs

Card / Loan	Balance	Interest rate	Annual interest (balance x interest rate)	Annual fee	Total cost (annual interest + annual fee)
	$____	___%	$_____	$____	$_____
	$____	___%	$_____	$____	$_____
	$____	___%	$_____	$____	$_____
	$____	___%	$_____	$____	$_____
	$____	___%	$_____	$____	$_____
Total annual cost					$_____
Total monthly cost (total annual cost ÷ 12)					$_____
Total weekly cost (total annual cost ÷ 52)					$_____

Now you know what it is costing you simply to maintain your current level of debt on an annual, monthly and weekly basis, you can start to think about whether or not your current level of repayments is going to get you out of the red and back into the black.

Minimum repayments don't shift debt

Somewhere on your monthly credit card statements you'll find a minimum repayment amount given. It is always fairly small in relation to the card balance, guaranteeing that it would take a very long time to repay the debt if we only ever made the minimum repayments. But how long? The minimum repayment is usually calculated as the interest amount charged plus about 1 per cent of the card balance. An online calculator can be used to work out how long it will take to reduce debt. As an example, a credit card debt of $6000 with a minimum monthly repayment of $150 will take just under 25 years to repay in full! And during that period an additional $8250 in interest will have been paid — that's considerably more than the original debt.

Shift your thinking, shift your debt

The fact is that all this personal debt can often be repaid within a short period of time, say in six or twelve months, depending on the level of debt and our salary, of course. The point, though, is that more often than not the debt that we find so embarrassing and stressful and that we have been holding on to for years, preventing us from accumulating any form of wealth, could actually be repaid very quickly. All we need is a little planning, followed by some hard work and discipline.

Exercise: Savings visualisation

Let's do a short exercise. Visualisation is a very powerful tool. Envisaging a goal can play an important role in the process of achieving it. We will discuss the setting of goals later in the book, but for now we'll start by imagining what it would be like simply to have a savings goal, and we'll break it down into three steps:

Step 1. Imagine that today your finances stand at zero. You have no wealth, but you also have no debt.

Step 2. Based on your current salary and your basic living costs (including mortgage or rent payments), set yourself a short-term savings goal. Imagine a sum of money you could put aside each week, to give you something to work towards.

Step 3. Think about the savings goal you might eventually build up to over the next five and ten years.

Whatever the goal you decided on in this exercise, however large or small the figure you settled on, I'm confident it would not have been $0. Hang on to that thought. If you are in a situation where you're burdened with what feels like unmanageable debt, you'll find, as you work your way through this book, that there is light at the end of the tunnel after all, that anything is possible.

To put it simply, if you currently have a personal debt burden that you have carried for a sustained period of time and that was incurred for no other reason than to facilitate your chosen lifestyle, then it is likely you are in this situation—aiming for zero, nothing, *nada*. It's time to change this, to start believing in yourself, to believe that you have the ability to lift your game, to change your behaviour and start thinking bigger.

Anyone can reduce their personal debt to zero, and from there the sky is the limit—our goals can continue to grow along with our wealth. We can start today with a clean slate and make the conscious decision to stop aiming for nothing, to start moving forward.

My brush with debt

Returning to my own personal story, as touched on in chapter 1, after my working holiday I came home with a $4000 credit card debt and felt the weight of the world on my shoulders. Even while backpacking around Europe I would lie awake at night, stressing about how I would ever repay my increasing debt. It felt like so much money to me, especially when I considered that $4000 was the most I had ever saved, and that had been to buy my air ticket and move to London.

After a couple of weeks in London I had already spent the money I'd arrived with and had only just begun working in the bar job. Over the next few months I saved as much as I could and booked a trip around Europe with the girlfriend I had come to meet in London. She was itching to go as she had already been working in the UK for almost six months. We agreed on a date to set off on our adventure that really didn't give me enough time to save properly.

Halfway through the trip, as my brand-new, for-emergencies-only credit card was racking up additional expenses, I was really stressed out. I knew deep down that I hadn't saved enough money for the trip. I also knew that I should have worked for longer in London before beginning my backpacking adventure, but I didn't want to admit it to myself. I was in serious denial. Years later I found the diary I had kept during this period, and it was a shock to read back over it and reflect on how much I had blamed everything and everyone but myself for the debt I was in. I desperately wanted it to be someone else's fault—the bank shouldn't have approved that level of credit, Europe was just *so* expensive! Eventually, on a train crossing Austria, I faced up to the reality that placing blame for my maxed-out credit card wasn't going to get me out of debt. I simply had to take action.

I headed back to London for a brief few days, and before I got on the flight home to Australia I made contact with my previous employer and arranged to start working with them again. My first shift was the day after I arrived back in the country, and from then on I took on as many shifts as I could and immediately applied for other work. I got a job in a pub, where I was rostered on during the afternoons and early evenings, and a week or so later I found another position in a bar that opened late on Friday and Saturday nights.

I had decided to move back to Melbourne to study. I knew I would need some savings behind me, and I was determined to repay my credit card debt in full before I left Brisbane. For the next six months I worked almost every day and survived on very little sleep, but I paid off my entire debt and saved the money I needed to make the move interstate.

Making it happen

Reflecting on this time now, I recognise it was a pretty insignificant sacrifice to have made to free myself from debt and stress and to build up a little savings to set me up in a new city. In any case, I loved my jobs and had a great time working as a bartender. I can't remember exactly how much I was earning an hour but it certainly wasn't a lot! It didn't matter though, because working so much meant I didn't have any time left over to go out and spend money. I had fun, stayed very focused, and as a result succeeded in freeing myself from debt and building up a small savings balance.

Short-term sacrifices

By making short-term sacrifices we can usually gain substantial benefits over the longer term. I learned this lesson at an early age, took responsibility for my problem and resolved it, which meant I was in a position to move forward financially. Had I not made that sacrifice at the time, who knows what situation I might be in now. Perhaps I would still have unresolved credit card debts holding me back.

Even though a year or so might feel like a long time to cut back on your spending or to work extra hours, the time will pass before you know it. In the meantime you will have been able to repay debt or build up your savings. The short-term sacrifice is totally worth it.

Long-term sacrifices

In Australia we are lucky. With social institutions such as the minimum wage laws, most of us are able to earn a fair level of remuneration in return for the employment we undertake. With this advantage we are generally in a position to prosper. This is not the case in many other countries around the world. I am always amazed by the adversity people are able to overcome in order to get what they need. I find inspiration in the story of a young Vietnamese girl who worked for me when we started Wealth Enhancers.

Tina decided in her early teenage years that she wanted to move to Australia, go to university and ultimately apply for citizenship so she could live here long term. She discussed the idea with her parents. They agreed that it would open up excellent opportunities for her and promised to do all they could to support her on her journey. As a family, they would save the money she would need. In the meantime Tina worked very hard at school and gained the grades she needed: she was accepted by RMIT University to study in Melbourne.

The cost for her family of sending Tina to Australia was very high: their sacrifice essentially eliminated their life savings. International student fees are much higher than the fees we pay as locals, and setting up a home in a new country with no support networks is also costly. As much as they would have liked to, Tina's parents could not afford to send her younger sister to Australia to follow the same path. Instead, Tina herself is taking responsibility for her younger sister. Now she has finished her university degree and has begun working full time, she is saving every cent she earns so she can provide her little sister with the same opportunity she had.

Tina shares a small apartment with a friend and never spends a dollar frivolously. Although she is not yet earning a large salary she has no debt, is paying her way through her CPA course, and has established a savings account that will be used to cover the costs of bringing her sister to Australia and paying for her university education.

I believe the strength to make sacrifices is in all of us. If we want something badly enough, we can find a way to make it happen. The problem is, many of us put off taking action and instead accept mediocrity, persuading ourselves that any time we really needed to we could repay our debt and get things sorted. But why wait? Why not just set a little aside each week starting today and begin repaying that useless debt now, so we can start building real wealth sooner. This means we'll have choices and the freedom to live life our own way.

Getting it under control

Probably the worst thing about personal debt is the control it can have over us. Beyond the obvious things like stress, and the inability to do the things we would like to do because of lack of funds, there are other, even more concerning issues to consider, such as our credit history, which can reduce our access to further credit such as a home loan. Missing the minimum credit card payments, and failing to make other bill payments, can result in an impaired credit history. The more often this happens, and the longer the missed payments drag on, the worse your credit history will become.

How does credit history work?

In Australia, individuals don't have an actual credit rating, as is commonly believed. However, a number of credit reporting agencies collect and hold information relating to our borrowing and credit history. These agencies can then provide a credit report on an individual upon request by an organisation such as a bank. We must give permission for that organisation to perform a credit check, but this is usually triggered when we complete an application form for credit of some kind. It is our choice whether or not to allow the provider to perform the credit check; however, it is unlikely a lender will grant us credit if we deny them this information.

The information kept by a credit reporting agency cannot be personal or discriminatory in nature and typically includes the following:

- identification information
- details of previous applications for credit
- details of current credit accounts
- court orders issued in the previous five years
- bankruptcy records for the previous seven years
- debts over $100 that are 60 days or more overdue.

If you are worried about what might be contained in your credit report, you can request that a copy be posted to you at no cost, or for a fee you can access it online from www.mycreditfile.com.au, which is part of the Veda Group, the main credit reporting agency in Australia, although there are others.

If your credit report contains information that indicates you are not financially reliable, you may be denied credit. All credit providers will base their decision on their own lending criteria, and your credit report will form only part of the application assessment process.

Pay those bills!

As we have seen, small repayment defaults in the short term are not worth the headaches they can cause later, when we may be in a far better financial position and are applying for a home loan or a lease agreement. So it's important always to pay your bills on time, even if you are making only minimum repayments. If this is not possible, calling the company to request an extension could avoid a negative entry being stored by a credit reporting agency.

Case study: Geoff's credit control deficit

After living in London for a couple of years, Geoff found himself in a situation where his personal debt prevented him from being able to return home to Australia when he eventually wanted to. Because his parents were born in the UK he had a British passport, so when money got a little tight following a trip around Europe Geoff applied for a local credit card. He thought he'd just use the funds to get him through the next few months, but he quickly racked up a substantial debt on the card.

With the downturn in employment following the GFC, the freelance work he'd been relying on was arriving far more slowly than it had been in the past and Geoff was unable to get on top of his credit card debt. So he started dipping into his Australian credit card, hoping to get back on top of it when work picked up. This became a bit of a bad habit. While trying to experience the once-in-a-lifetime opportunity of living in London, Geoff was now barely keeping his head above water financially. In an effort to get his finances back under control, Geoff made a decision to roll over his spiralling credit card debt into a personal loan arranged by his UK bank. After three years overseas, he really wanted to return home to Australia, but he felt completely trapped by his personal debt.

It would be almost two more years before Geoff finally came home, and he still had that personal loan, although he had reduced the balance owing a little. Since his return he has worked hard on his financial situation and he is starting to see some positive improvement.

The craziest thing about Geoff's situation was that in the end he didn't get to travel anywhere near as much as he'd hoped to. In all his years overseas he had managed only a couple of other weekend trips after that first, financially draining trip around Europe.

This is a good example of how overspending in the short term can have serious negative impacts over the long term, and the longer we leave it before addressing the situation, the bigger the problem becomes. Now is as good a time as any to start putting one foot in front of the other in the right direction. Just remember, by starting small, but starting now, you are taking back control of your personal financial situation.

Exercise: Get back to your roots

If you identify with this story, you might still be having trouble working out how you will be able to repay your debt and get back to zero so you can start thinking bigger and growing your wealth. As a starting point, try thinking back to your very first job.

Write down how much you earned each week, and below that figure make a list of the things you used to do to make that money stretch and last. You barely survived from week to week, I'm sure, but you did it, and you probably had a lot of fun. List all the fun and creative ways you and your friends found to have a good time on very limited financial resources.

Commonly, as our salary increases our expenses expand to match that salary and we don't make the financial gains we could. Compare the figure you wrote above with what you earn today, and ask yourself if you are maximising the gap. Well, now is the time to change that.

Starting today, set aside a percentage of your current weekly salary, start with 10 per cent—or be bold, why not 20 per cent? Look at the figure left over. Ask yourself, if you had no choice, could you survive on that amount each week? If the answer is yes, then start this week by applying the amount you have set aside from your salary to your debt (or put it in a savings account if you don't currently have any debt).

This is a really simple exercise to get you thinking. Later we will go through some specific ways to reduce personal debt as a part of your personal financial plan. In the following chapter we examine the nature of debt, and distinguish between debt to avoid and borrowing to help build wealth.

Key points

→ Aiming to be debt free is aiming for 'nothing' or zero.

→ Minimum credit card repayments will take 25 years to repay in full.

→ A short-term sacrifice now will pay off quicker than you think.

→ Don't let your debt control you; get back in control of your finances, starting now.

Putting it into action

Determine your debt

Write a list of all your personal debts, such as credit cards and personal loans (see table 3.3), and determine exactly how much you owe. (Use table 3.2 on p. 29, which we completed earlier, to tally it all up.)

Table 3.3: my personal debts

Source	Amount
Credit card	–$_____
Credit card	–$_____
Personal loan	–$_____
Car loan	–$_____
Total	–$_____

We will be completing a full budget later in the book, but for now establish a direct debit for each pay cycle and allocate an additional 10 to 20 per cent of your salary to repaying your debt. Of course, it's important to be sure you are meeting all of your minimum repayments to avoid late fees and a poor credit record, so don't make changes to your current repayment rates, other than to increase them.

Read your statements!

From now on each month it's important that you read your credit card statements in full. This will remind you of all the reasons why you need to reduce your personal debt, and will help you stay focused as you watch the balance come down over time.

CHAPTER 4

Good debt, **bad** debt

*Debt is like any other trap, easy enough to get into,
but hard enough to get out of.*

Henry Wheeler Shaw

In chapter 2 we talked about how important it is to take control of our financial situation, and in particular to start paying off any personal debt we may have. But not all debt is bad. In fact, some debt can be a good thing, as it offers us greater exposure to an investment sooner than we would otherwise be able to achieve. Quite simply, if we had to pay for a property in full with our savings, there would be far fewer homeowners in Australia. So it's a matter of understanding when we should borrow for something and when we shouldn't. We need to understand when debt is beneficial to us and when it is detrimental, because there isn't much middle ground.

Borrowing effectively—the basics

It's actually fairly simple. Good debt relates to funds borrowed to purchase an asset that will likely go up in value and may also provide income. With bad debt, the amount borrowed is used to fund lifestyle expenses (such as putting clothes or a holiday on a credit card) or to purchase an asset that will decrease in value (such as a car). What we should always keep in mind is that if we ever needed to we could sell our assets and repay all our debts in full, hopefully with something left over.

The other advantage of borrowing money to invest in an asset such as shares or property is that the interest is tax deductible. (It is important to note that the interest on a home loan for a house we live in—our primary residence—is not tax deductible, but we will return to this point later.) On the other hand, interest on credit cards, personal loans, or any other debts not used for investment purposes, is absolutely not tax deductible.

Borrowing thumbs-up

Things that are okay to borrow money for include:

- a property
- a share portfolio or managed fund
- a business (provided you have a sound business plan and have sought legal advice).

Gearing up

When borrowing to invest in one of the types of assets listed above, we combine our personal savings with borrowed money in order to build a larger share portfolio or purchase a property. This is referred to as leveraging or gearing. Gearing is further defined as positive, negative or neutral. These are actually fairly simple distinctions to do with whether the underlying investment is generating a profit, breaking even or costing us money. None of these situations is necessarily good or bad in itself, but to determine the best way to structure the debt on an investment asset it is important to understand the differences and consider what we are trying to achieve.

A *positively geared* asset is one that is generating income (either through rent, interest or dividends) in excess of the interest payable on the loan. This means we have money in our pockets at the end of the financial year, and this surplus is taxable. A *neutrally geared* asset is one that is generating income (through rent, interest or dividends) that is equivalent to the interest payable on the loan, therefore negating any positive or negative impact. A *negatively geared* asset is one that is generating income (through rent, interest or dividends) that is less than that of the interest payable on the loan. This means we qualify for a tax deduction for the loss we have made.

Gearing is further defined by the ratio of debts to assets that it represents. It is generally not a good idea to borrow 100 per cent of the cost price of any of these assets, unless you own a lot of other assets in full, as the value of any investment can fluctuate. You may have heard the term 'gearing ratio' before. It essentially refers to the amount of debt in relation to the value of the asset. If you save up a 20 per cent deposit for your first home and borrow the remainder you have a gearing ratio of 80 per cent.

The 30 per cent benchmark

A good overall gearing ratio to aim for is around 30 per cent. This means if you add up everything you own, then calculate your total debt as a percentage of that and come up with a figure of 30 per cent, you're geared at an optimal level. Why? Because 30 per cent represents a very safe level of debt, in that it would be highly unlikely that the value of all of your assets would decline to below 30 per cent of their current value. This means you are borrowing enough to gain further exposure to grow your wealth, but not so much that you are taking on risk that your assets will be worth less than your debt.

In reality, though, in some periods in our lives our gearing ratio will be higher than in others. Commonly, when we are younger and building wealth our gearing ratio will be quite high, and over time, as we start to accumulate more and repay debt, our gearing ratio will fall.

Young people in Australia who rush headlong into purchasing a property are typically geared at around 80 to 90 per cent, or even higher. So your gearing ratio throughout your life will fluctuate, but the 30 per cent benchmark gives you something comfortable to aim for.

Sustainable debt

None of these circumstances change the fact that it is a good idea to borrow to invest (or invest at all for that matter) only in an asset that we believe will increase in value over time. Otherwise it is not really an asset.

Negatively geared property was very popular throughout the noughties, when people were completely comfortable with losing money year on year in order to gain a tax deduction for their losses. The reason why they felt comfortable with this was that property prices were on the rise and the losses sustained each year could be more than made up for when the property was later sold.

This approach is not sustainable and could only really be relied upon if we had a crystal ball to tell us exactly when markets were going to go up or down. Nonetheless, a sensible level of debt used to purchase assets such as property and shares that will almost certainly ultimately trend upwards can form an important part of our wealth creation strategy.

Borrowing to build wealth— home loans

Borrowing for anything that is likely to increase in value, such as property or shares, is acceptable provided we put a plan and some guidelines in place. The idea behind borrowing to purchase a property is that the value of the property will increase over time as the loan is repaid, ultimately leaving us with an asset that we own outright, that continues to increase in value and that can one day be sold to realise this value.

First save the deposit

Property is generally a high-cost asset, and most young people would be hard pressed to save up for such a purchase if they were completely reliant on their own money. They should instead aim to save at least 20 per cent to cover the deposit and then apply to a lending institution to borrow the rest. This will still mean a hefty loan but will avoid additional costs such as mortgage insurance, which is payable in the event of a loan being taken out for more than 80 per cent of a property's value.

Most home loans in Australia are established for a 30-year period, which means that if we stick to the minimum rate of repayment it will take us 30 years to pay off the loan. Interest rates can vary from time to time, and if we don't have a fixed-rate loan, this will mean that our minimum repayment rates will change too, increasing when interest rates go up and decreasing when they go down.

Set your borrowing limit, and stick to it!

To establish how much we should borrow (and therefore how much we should aim to save for a deposit and ultimately to spend on purchasing a property), we need to consider what we can afford to pay towards our mortgage each week after all our other living expenses have been covered. We can include our current rent in this amount if we're buying a property to move into. A good indication of affordability is the amount we are currently saving plus rent. There are a number of apps and online calculators to help you to determine the full cost of purchasing a property (including stamp duty) and to work out what the minimum repayments will be, based on the size of the loan.

Once we've set our limit on what we're willing to borrow in line with the minimum repayments we can afford, it's important we stick to that limit when we're out house hunting. If we can make additional repayments on our home loan, we'll be able to pay it off before the full 30-year term expires. Repaying our home loan sooner will also mean we pay less interest. Figure 4.1 shows how much time we can save by increasing our weekly loan repayments, assuming a loan of $500 000 at a rate of 6 per cent for 30 years.

Figure 4.1: time saved by increasing weekly loan repayments

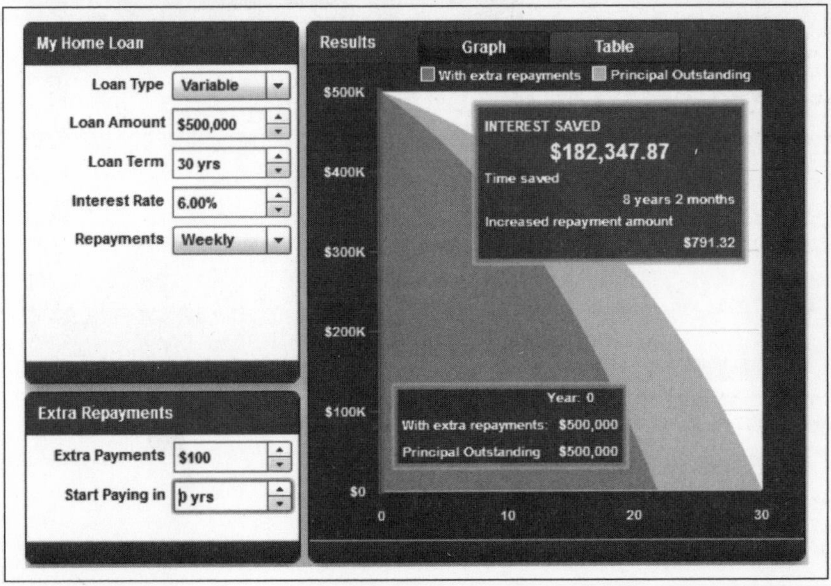

Source: © Infochoice.

The weekly minimum repayments are \$691.32, but if we can increase that by \$100 each week to \$791.32 we will save more than \$180 000 in interest payments as well as knocking eight years off the loan.

As we can see, we need to consider the details of the loan carefully to assess whether or not we can afford to meet our minimum repayments. The full purchase cost over the entire loan term is quite a lot more than we might think. Using the same example, if we kept our loan for the full 30 years and made only the minimum repayments, the total cost of the loan once all principal and interest repayments have been made amounts to \$1 078 452 (see figure 4.2), more than double the amount initially borrowed. It is likely that over a 30-year period the increased value of the property will more than compensate for this, but these are considerations that need to form part of the decision to buy a property.

Figure 4.2: total cost of loan based on minimum repayments

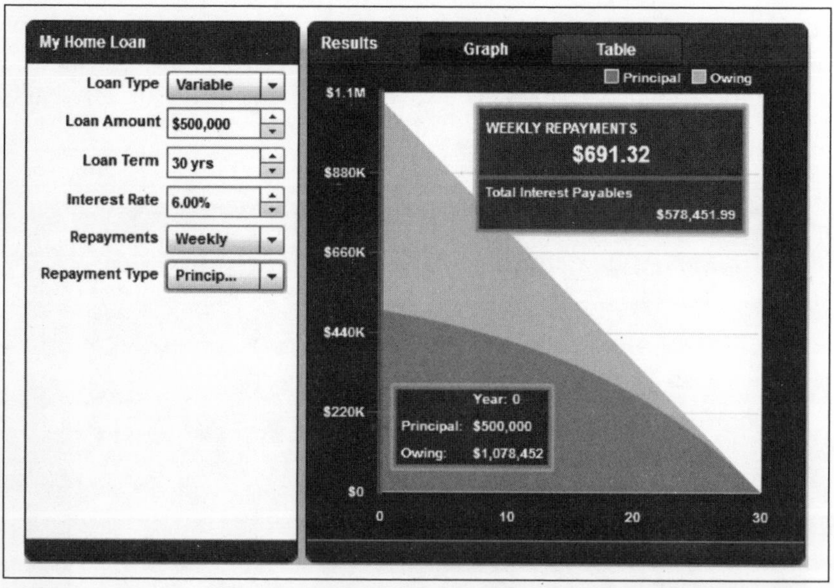

Source: © Infochoice.

Borrowing for shares

The advantage of borrowing to invest in shares or a managed fund is that the amount needn't be as high as borrowing to invest in property. In fact, if you plan to invest money of your own regularly to build up a larger share portfolio, you can often borrow as little as $1000. In most instances we don't repay the principal of the loan, simply the interest being incurred, which would be offset by any income received from the shares (known as dividends).

We will learn more about the characteristics of shares and property as investment vehicles later. Essentially, though, both forms of investment have the same overall objective: to create wealth through the investments' increasing in value over time.

Keep gearing levels low

Shares can generate income as well as increase in value. Using a loan to purchase shares is a great way to secure a larger number of shares than we would be able to buy outright. Obviously, there is a risk that the value of the shares can drop below that of the loan balance. Before the GFC many people took out large loans to invest in shares, which they purchased with 100 per cent borrowed money, contributing none of their own. Then when sharemarkets took a turn south, they were left with share portfolios worth less than their loans.

Property markets too have been hit in recent times. Market conditions can impact on any investment, which is why it is always a good idea to keep our gearing levels low to avoid a situation where our underlying investments are worth less than what we paid for them. Even then, history tells us, values will most often pick up again eventually, so if we do not need to sell the investments it might be wise to hold on to them. The problem is coping with the market volatility in the meantime.

Borrowing thumbs-down

Things that are *not* okay to borrow money for include:

- holidays
- a car

- shopping, partying or other lifestyle expenses
- elective surgery, furniture, electrical goods and a myriad other products for which finance is offered.

Do you deserve it?

There is no reason to believe we deserve to buy anything, ever, unless we have worked hard and saved our money for it. We live in a world of instant gratification, and it's hard to resist the urge to pull out the plastic every time we really want something, but practising delayed gratification is so much more rewarding. We just need to change our habits and mindset, to get used to the idea that if we want something we may just need to wait until we can afford it.

The slow money rule: If we don't have the money, we can't buy it.

This said, the use of credit cards or interest-free loans is not always a bad thing. If we are disciplined and use these credit facilities wisely, they are actually a great way to use someone else's money to achieve more for ourselves. It's important to be aware, though, that generally these products are designed for, and targeted towards, those who do not manage their money well. If we are disciplined with our money, and understand the reasons why paying interest on these types of expenses is a bad idea, we can make these products work for us.

Using a credit card effectively

Credit cards come with plenty of enticements, such as frequent flyer points, gift cards, travel insurance and more. They also specify a period of time, which can be up to 55 days, during which our purchases will incur no interest.

The slow money rule: If the card is paid off in full before the due date on the bill, no interest is incurred.

So if we are disciplined enough to limit our spending to what we can afford, and make a full repayment each month before the due date, the positive power of credit cards is within our reach.

Think about it. If our regular salary is sitting in a high-interest savings account all month while we are spending the bank's money through the credit card, then we are using the bank's money for free while our own money earns interest. But remember, the rate of interest charged on our credit card will often be more than four times what we would earn in a high-interest savings account, so we need to be 100 per cent organised and be sure to get that debt paid in full before the due date.

Table 4.1 shows how someone with $4000 of monthly expenses can gain more than $300 in interest income in a year simply by paying for these expenses by credit and leaving the $4000 in a high-interest savings account. The $4000 will need to be used at the end of each 55-day period, but in the meantime it is earning interest. I have used an interest rate of 5 per cent in this example.

Table 4.1: annual interest income accrued by paying monthly expenses by credit card

Month	Income	Credit card payment	Interest received
January	$4000		$30
February	$4000	−$4000	$30
March	$4000	−$4000	$30
April	$4000	−$4000	$30
May	$4000	−$4000	$30
June	$4000	−$4000	$30
July	$4000	−$4000	$30
August	$4000	−$4000	$30
September	$4000	−$4000	$30
October	$4000	−$4000	$30
November	$4000	−$4000	$30
December	$4000	−$4000	$30
Total interest received			**$360**

Beyond financial benefits

Another advantage of using a credit card properly to cover our expenses is the rewards program that often forms part of the credit card package. Rewards programs usually involve some kind of point collection system, in which accumulated points can then be 'cashed in' for a product or service. These programs vary substantially across different credit card products, but it is common for one point to be earned for every dollar spent. Frequent flyer programs are an example of these rewards: we'll often earn enough frequent flyer points for a free domestic flight each year, or perhaps even an international flight.

Many credit cards also offer complimentary travel insurance, which can be a great benefit for those of us who travel frequently. It's of course important to check the policy in detail to be sure it meets our needs.

When we put all of these benefits together, including the additional interest income, rewards programs and travel insurance, we're already ahead of the game.

Beware of the annual card fee

There is one other thing we need to be aware of when choosing a credit card: always check the annual fee, because if the level of the fee starts to outweigh the benefits then it won't be worthwhile. Some credit cards incur no annual fee. One of these that also has a rewards program could be ideal, although there are many products available with annual fees ranging between $0 and $100, which is a good range to stay within. The strategy illustrated in table 4.1 (on p.47) would probably still pay off provided the annual fee was below $362. Any higher and it might not be worthwhile.

Using interest-free finance

We've all moved house at some stage, requiring us to buy costly items such as furniture and appliances. A new fridge, washer and dryer, for example, can easily set us back $2500. Often furniture and appliance stores offer interest-free loan terms of 24 or 36 months, sometimes even longer. If we've already saved the money needed, though, we wouldn't normally think to take up such an offer.

Well, guess what? By having money in the bank we are perfectly placed to take advantage of these interest-free offers—first, because we are in a strong position to be granted the credit required and, second, because we can put our money to work for us right away instead of simply spending it. Think of it this way: Right now our $2500 is worth exactly $2500. That means we can buy $2500 worth of goods or services with our money now. Over time, though, as a result of inflation our $2500 may buy us only the equivalent of what $2100 would buy today.

If we take up the 24-months interest-free terms, make the minimum repayment due each month and in the final month ensure we repay the remaining debt in full, we can put our money to work elsewhere, starting today. We'll gain from the benefit of inflation (we're already almost $400 ahead). Meanwhile our $2500 has been earning interest for two years (adding another $150 or so), so we're now up by $550 and have essentially secured ourselves a fridge, washer and dryer at a 20 per cent discount.

Of course, should we miss full repayment by even one day at the end of the interest-free period, we risk being charged interest all the way back to the start date, usually at an exorbitantly high rate. So we need to be very careful to ensure that the entire loan is repaid and the account closed before the end of the loan term.

Before deciding whether to sign up for one of these interest-free offers:

- check the annual or monthly fee associated with the credit facility
- ask what kind of discount they can apply if you pay cash today (sometimes this will be more beneficial).

This purchase strategy is just another way we can make short-term personal debt work for us instead of against us.

The slow money rule: If you can't afford it, you can't have it.

Using credit card balance transfers effectively

A credit card balance transfer can be a great way to reduce credit card debt quickly. To attract new customers, lenders in Australia frequently introduce special deals under which we can transfer the balance of one of our credit cards to another lender in return for an interest-free period or a period at a substantially reduced interest rate. Typically such a deal will offer no interest for six months, at which time the usual high interest will again be charged. Sometimes low rates such as 2 to 3 per cent will be available for a period of up to a year. It's important to check out any annual card fees that may be applicable and to look for one with a very low fee. Moving money around through a series of such balance transfers can help us to repay debt much faster because we get a break from paying interest.

Applying for a balance transfer is similar to applying for a new credit card, so the application process could be blocked by a negative credit rating report. However, if you are approved and manage to transfer your entire credit card balance to a new interest-free environment, you will have the opportunity to make serious headway in repaying your balance over the six-month period.

Tables 4.2 and 4.3 show the difference between using a balance transfer and simply trying to repay your card while still earning interest.

Table 4.2: credit card repayments over 12 months at 18 per cent interest

Month	Balance	Repayment	Interest
January	$5000	$450	$68
February	$4618	$450	$63
March	$4231	$450	$57
April	$3837	$450	$51
May	$3438	$450	$45
June	$3033	$450	$39
July	$2622	$450	$33
August	$2204	$450	$26
September	$1781	$450	$20

Month	Balance	Repayment	Interest
October	$1351	$450	$14
November	$914	$450	$7
December	$471	$450	$0
Total interest paid			**$423**

Table 4.3: credit card repayments over 12 months at no interest

Month	Balance	Repayment	Interest
January	$5000	$450	$0
February	$4550	$450	$0
March	$4100	$450	$0
April	$3650	$450	$0
May	$3200	$450	$0
June	$2750	$450	$0
July	$2300	$450	$0
August	$1850	$450	$0
September	$1400	$450	$0
October	$950	$450	$0
November	$500	$450	$0
December	$50	$450	$0
Total interest paid			**$0**

We can see that by using a 12-month balance transfer, we can pay off the credit card balance a full month earlier than if interest is being charged at a rate of 18 per cent for the whole year. This can be a really effective way to reduce credit card debt if we are committed to it. It's most important, though, to cancel any old credit cards once the new one has been issued and the balance transferred.

It's also a great idea to repeat the process with another lender when the initial balance transfer period has run out. This way we can keep moving credit around in an interest-free environment until we have managed to repay it in full. Although this may seem like a lot of work, it will save us money and help us stay focused on reducing our debt.

Borrowing to purchase a car

When is it okay to borrow to purchase a car? Actually, never! Why? Because a car goes down in value the moment we drive it out of the dealership, and it costs a lot to maintain, insure and run each year. Also, the interest on the loan is not tax deductible. Essentially, cars decrease in value, produce no income and incur high maintenance costs, so they are not assets, as we usually understand them, but liabilities.

Unfortunately, most of us think it's normal to take out a loan to purchase a car. Many of my clients are repaying a car loan, and in most cases, because of the speed at which cars deteriorate in value, this debt is higher than the value of the car if they were to sell it today. And it doesn't take long to reach this point if you borrow most or all of the cost of the vehicle.

Case study: Christian's expensive lesson

Christian had bought himself a $25 000 car for his 25th birthday—$1000 for every year he'd been alive. He didn't really have any savings. It was a spur-of-the-moment purchase, because he was sick of driving around the old bomb he'd had for many years and wanted something he felt matched his current lifestyle. He had a decent job and was starting to earn good money, so he knew he could afford the monthly repayments of $400. He'd worked hard for a couple of years and he felt he deserved the reward.

In reality, he simply hadn't spent the time saving the money he needed to make such a large purchase. Because he hadn't saved anything at all, he applied for full 100 per cent finance with no deposit required. The loan was approved and off Christian drove feeling great about his new wheels.

Four years later, when the car was a little older but still looking nice, Christian decided to travel overseas on a working holiday. He quit his job, packed everything up and put his car on the market. He eventually sold the car, after spending $2200 on repairs and maintenance to obtain a roadworthy certificate, for $9000. It was substantially less than what he had listed it for, and what he expected, but he had to live with it. But it got worse. At the time of the sale the loan balance stood at just over $15 000. Once he had applied the $9000 from the sale he still owed $6000 on his original loan. With no spare cash to clear the debt, Christian had to make provision for continuing the repayments throughout his time overseas and it was a further three years before it was completely repaid.

In any other situation, Christian might not have sold the car but simply kept it until the loan was paid off, but his heart had been set on spending time overseas. So he learned a painful and very expensive lesson, first on how quickly and how much a car can reduce in value, and second on how long it can take and how much it will cost to repay such a substantial loan in full.

Table 4.4 shows what the car cost Christian over the four years he owned it.

Table 4.4: Christian's car purchase—the full picture

Costs	$
Purchase price	$25 000
Loan amount (at 9% interest)	$25 000
Interest charged (over 7 years)	$8 800
Roadworthy repairs prior to sale	$2 200
Total cost of car	$36 000
Less sale price received	−$9 000
Net cost of the car	$27 000
Cost per month during period of use	$563

Christian spent $27 000 over seven years, although he got to drive the car for only three years, and he came away with nothing. And this figure doesn't include the additional expenses associated with owning a car including fuel, maintenance and insurances.

The never-ending car loan

Christian found that having a car loan hadn't benefited him at all. He learned that had he saved the money for the car first, he would still have lost money at the time of sale, but he would have come away with $9000, which was essentially the amount he paid in interest over the years. He also wouldn't have been burdened with an outstanding debt while he was overseas.

Many people who haven't learned the hard lesson Christian did end up in a situation that I refer to as the never-ending car loan! It usually starts with our first car and a small loan (say, $3000) associated with it. A couple of years later the small loan has been paid off but we're sick of driving that little 'bomb' around, so we happily sign the paperwork on a trade-in (maybe $500) for a $10 000 car, and a $9500 loan.

This car seems pretty nice at first, but after four or five years, when the loan is *almost* paid off, we start feeling like we deserve to be driving something a little bit better. We're now earning more, so surely we can afford something nice, maybe even something brand new. After a few trips around the car yards, we strike a great deal, trading in the old beast for $4000 and taking possession of a brand-new car—only $32 000 fully financed.

And as the cycle continues to repeat itself, we pay (with hefty interest) car loan after car loan, often soaking up our spare monthly cash, which could have been used to begin an investment program and really build something.

So what's the alternative?

Hopefully by now we're all convinced that car loans are not a good idea. Far better to buy a cheap car to get us around for a couple of years while we save our money. If we set aside the $500 a month we would have spent on car loan repayments, it will take us less than two years to save $10 000, and then we'll be able to trade in for that better car.

If we continue to do this, increasing our savings a little each year, it won't be long before we're in a position to buy an even better, almost new car. Buying an almost new car is a smart thing to do: a one- or two-year-old car will have dropped substantially in value from its initial purchase price but will still have that brand-new feel. Most car models change shape significantly only every few years, so there'll probably be no major difference between that almost new car and a new one, other than the much-reduced price tag.

So if you currently have a car loan, one of the most important things you can do is to focus on paying it off, and then keeping the car for at least a couple of years before upgrading. When you do manage to pay off the loan in full, start putting the same amount aside as you were previously paying in repayments and build up a savings account that you will be able to use when you do buy another car. That way you will break the cycle and won't need to enter into any further loan contracts for vehicles.

The right debt

As we can see, debt does have a place in our wealth creation journey. What's important is that we use it to purchase assets that are likely to increase in value, rather than to fund our lifestyle or buy things that will only fall in value over time. In a society in which credit is very easy to come by, it can be hard at times to exercise this level of discipline when it seems that everyone around us has everything they want, and they have it now. But, as we saw in the previous chapter, a little sacrifice now will pay dividends in the future. When we step off the debt bus and onto the savings bus our destination becomes a whole lot more exciting, because we are beginning to actually build something instead of just chasing our tails.

In chapter 5 we explore the central role of time in our wealth creation journey, paradoxically both as the one variable we can't beat and as a powerful agent to harness for our advantage.

Key points

→ Good debt is used to grow wealth; bad debt is used to fund a lifestyle we can't yet afford.

→ Always have a plan and determine the repayments you can afford before borrowing.

→ Credit cards and interest-free deals can work in our favour if we use them wisely.

→ Car loans are bad news.

Putting it into action

Do you have personal debt or credit card debt? If so, it's time to get rid of it once and for all. Jump online and search for balance transfers that may be available to you. Look for one that has a low rate of interest (0 per cent if possible) and a low annual card fee (ensure it is lower than your current card—under $100 is ideal). Apply for a balance transfer and when it is approved, cancel your old credit card and start repaying your debt as quickly as possible. The best way is to divide the total debt by the number of months you have at a low or no interest rate, and aim to pay off this figure each month.

CHAPTER 5

Start
yesterday

Every journey starts with a single step.

Confucius

People often tell me they'd really like to come and see me for advice — once they've got some money in the bank. Why do they put it off? Some people assume that financial advisers are concerned only about looking after their clients' investments. But that's not really what we're about at all. A good financial adviser will help you identify what is fundamentally important to you and what your goals are, then help you to pursue your passion by developing a plan and then keeping you on track and accountable.

Others think it would be too embarrassing to admit to their personal debts and financial muddle, and imagine they'll sort it out for themselves first. This doesn't really make sense either, though — it's like deciding to clean the house before the cleaner comes. If we look at the psychology behind it, it is just the kind of behaviour that has got them into the situation they are in in the first place. It's about saving face and keeping up appearances.

Now is the time

Now is the perfect time to start looking after your finances and taking responsibility for how you spend and save your hard-earned money. Don't delay. You really need to start getting on top of things, little by little, immediately. If, after all you've read so far, you still aren't feeling motivated enough to take the plunge, this simple exercise I came across in *The Barefoot Investor* ebook might help give you some perspective.

Exercise: The income sink hole

Think about how much you've earned, on average, over your working life to date. Come up with an approximate annual figure, then multiply that figure by the number of years you've been working. See table 5.1.

Table 5.1: the sink hole

Average annual income	Years worked	Approximate total earned
$_____	_____ years	= $_____

Now reflect on that number and ask yourself, 'Where *is* all that money?'

Some of us may well be in a good financial position, with some wealth built up, in which case we should pat ourselves on the back and keep reading, so we can learn how to take it to the next level. Others of us may have nothing to show for the passage of years, or may even be in the red, with credit cards, personal loans or other persistent debts and no significant assets. That's okay too though—we just have a little more work to do. Whatever the case, the good news is that it's never too late to start.

Obviously, very few people (if anyone at all) would be able to save 100 per cent of what they earn across their working life. However, the sooner we put our money to work for us by investing wisely or saving, the greater our wealth will become over time, because the longer your money is invested, the more time it will have to grow.

The power of time

Remember, time is the one variable that we just can't beat. It's on everyone's hit list, though! All the get-rich-quick schemes in the world exist purely to feed our desire to defy time, to achieve wealth quickly without investing the time and effort actually needed. Once we have accepted the fact that we can't beat time, by focusing on the power of starting small and starting now we can benefit enormously from time's special power.

When we invest in something for a sustained period of time, we start to benefit from the effects of compound interest. That means we will start to earn interest on top of the interest we've earned in the past. Compound interest is one of our most powerful allies when we invest or save regularly. Essentially it tips the odds in our favour. It is a lot harder to go wrong so long as we are putting money aside regularly in a savings account or an investment, and not drawing it back out again.

High-interest savings accounts

Let's look at an example. If we put $100 each week into an online savings account with an interest rate of 5 per cent, at the end of 12 months we will have invested $5200 but will have a balance of roughly $5435, including $235 in interest received. If, in the following year, we continue to put $100 each week into the same investment, we will have invested a total of $10 400, but our balance will stand at $11 043, including $643 in interest.

Let's assume we do exactly the same thing in the third year. We've now invested a total of $15 600, which has grown to $16 938 (see figure 5.1). By now we have received $1238 in interest.

Figure 5.1: compound interest accrued on a high-interest savings account

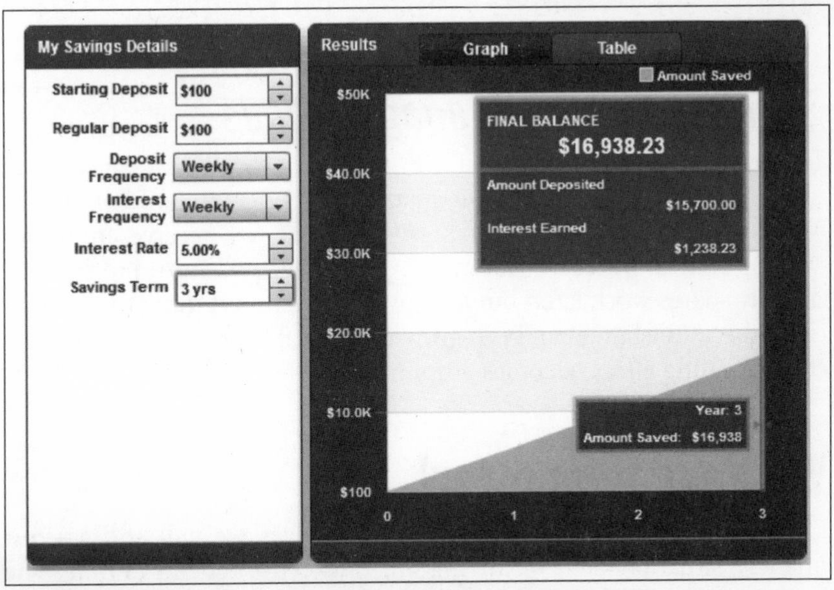

Source: © Infochoice.

As you can start to see, the effect of earning interest on top of interest is that our wealth starts to grow beyond simply what we are putting away each week. Table 5.2 shows how much you can expect to achieve over different time frames depending on how much you put aside each week, based on an interest rate of 5 per cent.

Table 5.2: interest accrual over 1–10 years

Weekly savings	1 year	2 years	3 years	4 years	5 years	10 years
$20	$1066	$2186	$3364	$4603	$5905	$13485
$50	$2665	$5466	$8411	$11507	$14761	$33713
$100	$5330	$10932	$16938	$23014	$29523	$67426
$150	$7994	$16398	$25233	$34521	$44284	$101139
$250	$13324	$27331	$42055	$57534	$73807	$168565
$400	$21318	$43729	$67288	$92055	$118090	$269703
$600	$31977	$65594	$100932	$138082	$177136	$404555
$1000	$53296	$109323	$168221	$230137	$295226	$674258

Share portfolio or managed funds

This effect can be increased if we invest in shares, especially if we utilise a dividend reinvestment plan. Dividend reinvestment simply means purchasing more shares with income we receive from our existing shares, instead of taking it as cash. We will learn more about the way shares work later, but for now the important thing to consider is that because shares can both grow in value and produce income, the compounding effect becomes amplified.

We have the power!

Every extra day we let go by, telling ourselves we will address our financial situation later, we are missing out on the benefits of time. The longer we persuade ourselves that we'll get on top of it soon, or that it'll sort itself out eventually, the bigger the figure of lost wealth that we calculated earlier grows.

We have the power to change our thinking to improve our financial situation and our lives. More importantly, *only* we have this power. We need to stop putting it off and take action today. As with any positive accomplishment in life, it all starts with the decision to act.

In part II we get smart by exploring the main investment vehicles available to us and assessing the part each can play in helping us to achieve our financial goals.

Key points

→ There is no time like the present, so get started today.

→ Remember, time is the one variable we can't control.

→ Regularly saving or investing even a little will add up to a lot over time, thanks to the power of compound interest.

Putting it into action

Start saving today! Even if you can only find $20 a week for now, it's a start. Search online for high-interest savings accounts. You'll find websites that compare the products currently available—there are plenty of options. Look for an account that has a high rate of interest and no account-keeping fees. It's also a good idea to establish an account with an institution other than the one you currently bank with. This reduces your opportunities to access your savings and dip into the account when you shouldn't.

Once you have established the account, set up a weekly automatic transfer starting *now*. Try not to look at your balance all the time, but set yourself a day each month to review it—and pat yourself on the back as it grows!

PART II

Let's
get
smart

CHAPTER 6

Many roads
to
wealth

Do not wait; the time will never be 'just right'. Start where you stand, and work with whatever tools you may have at your command, and better tools will be found as you go along.

Napoleon Hill

There are many ways we can build wealth. In my opinion, however, we Australians go about it completely the wrong way around. We looked at this idea in chapter 2 and I want to go through it again because I think it's important.

If we think about it, with such pressure to become homeowners, many young people are buying their first property before they have even acquired the skill to save cash in the bank. Scraping together the bare minimum deposit, or nothing at all, and applying for a 90 to 100 per cent home loan, incurring expensive mortgage insurance along the way, has become common.

As proud new homeowners we spend many years shackled to our mortgages, struggling with interest rate rises and finding it hard to make ends meet. Eventually, provided no major unexpected expenses (such as property maintenance costs) have arisen, things will start to look a little better, and perhaps we will consider establishing a share portfolio, but in many cases we're more inclined to jump straight into an investment property. All the while, we still don't have any cash in the bank.

What if we did things the other way around? In the following chapters we will go through the different ways we can create wealth, and then in part III we will consider some smarter ways to go about building a financially secure future.

Understanding investing

The first thing we need to understand, before we even start to learn more about the different types of investments available, is what exactly investing is and what the characteristics of an investment are. A dictionary definition of investment is 'placing of money or capital in something that gives returns, as interest or income, or appreciates in value'.

Basically, then, to invest is to put your money into something you believe will provide an increase in overall value at some time in the future. It is important to remember this rule whenever you are considering making an investment in something.

There are two ways an investment can create an increase in overall value: these are referred to as capital growth and income. Other important considerations in relation to investing are risk and liquidity. So the main characteristics of an investment are:

- capital
- income
- risk versus return
- liquidity.

Capital

Capital refers to the value of an asset we have invested in. It is the price we paid for the investment and the price for which we eventually sell the investment. The capital value of an investment can go up or down, depending on what price someone else is willing to buy the asset for when we decide to sell it. Generally speaking, with any investment we make we should be looking for something that will increase in value, or at the very least will not decrease in value.

Using property as an example, the capital value is the value of the property at the time it is bought or sold. The same principle applies to a diamond. The chances are that 10 years after we bought the diamond it would be worth a different amount if we were to sell it on the open market (hopefully it has increased in value!).

Determining the value of a listed asset, such as shares on the Australian Securities Exchange (ASX), is relatively straightforward. An unlisted asset requires a professional valuation, which would be partly based on recent sales of similar assets. Ultimately, though, the value of any asset is never known with certainty until an offer to purchase is made and agreed upon.

The slow money rule: An asset is only ever worth what someone else is willing to pay for it.

Income

Income refers to any money we receive that is generated from an investment we own. This income could vary from time to time and needs to be included in our taxable income when we lodge our annual tax return. The income received is taxed at our marginal tax rate, which is an important consideration when evaluating the return on our investment.

For an investment property, the income generated is the rent we receive from tenants. Over the long term it is likely that the rent will increase; however, it could also decrease or remain steady for a period. The diamond we bought 10 years ago did not generate any income during the period of ownership (unless of course we found a way to rent it out too!).

Some investments therefore have the characteristics of both capital growth and income, while some have just one of these characteristics. Neither is inherently better than the other. We need to consider our reasons for investing and our time frame. Table 6.1 (overleaf) shows some examples of assets, their characteristics and their uses.

Table 6.1: examples of assets

Type of asset	Characteristics	Example of use
Cash	No capital growth Produces income	Short-term savings goals (for example, a holiday). Could also be used to produce a secure income in retirement.
Shares	Capital growth Produces income	Medium- to long-term wealth creation. Could later be sold or income used to change careers, open a business or start a family.
Diamonds	Capital growth No income	Long-term wealth creation strategy, possibly to provide diversification away from listed assets in a retirement fund.
Property	Capital growth Produces income	Long-term wealth creation strategy. Usually mortgaged, so best used for capital growth to realise a large sum of money at some stage in the future.

The most important thing to consider before purchasing any investment is whether or not the overall investment return is likely to be positive. We will never know for sure, because all investments carry with them an element of risk, but we make our decision after carefully assessing all the available information.

An assessment of the total investment return of an asset we have sold will include the increase in capital value, plus any income received, less any associated expenses (such as tax or maintenance costs). If this produces a positive outcome, then we are on the right track.

The next step is to calculate that return as an annualised percentage in order to establish if it produced a good investment return in relation to the risk we took on. Table 6.2 shows the return achieved on a small share portfolio after taking into account all taxes, income and capital growth.

Table 6.2: investment return on a small share portfolio

	Value	Explanation
Total invested	$26 000	$100 each week for 5 years
Dividends received	$1 755	total dividends received over 5 years, not reinvested
Tax paid	–$527	tax paid on dividends over 5 years at 30 per cent
Sale price	**$38 760**	**value of shares when sold at end of 5 years**
Capital growth	$12 760	sale price less total invested over 5 years
CGT tax	–$1 914	tax paid on the capital growth
Net return	$12 075	total return including dividends and capital growth, less all taxes
Rate of return	**9.29%**	**annual return on investment achieved**

This turned out to be a good return on investment, a return we would have been unlikely to have achieved through investing in cash.

Risk versus return

Different investments will perform differently and show varying levels of volatility. Volatility refers to the frequency and extent of movement in the value of the asset, or the income the asset is producing, which determines the risk.

Generally, the lower the volatility associated with an asset, the lower the possible return or loss; and the higher the volatility, the higher the possible returns or losses. This relationship is referred to as *risk versus return*. So choosing an investment is also about choosing an investment that will achieve the return we need for the lowest level of risk possible, because volatility is what will make us uncomfortable and potentially want to sell the asset at the wrong time. We call this the *sleep at night factor*. It's is not worth investing in something that is going to keep you up all night worrying about it. This emotional situation can result in poor decisions being made.

Considering risk versus return will help us determine the right investment for the right goal, as we will discuss further in chapter 13. Working out what return we actually need to reach our goals is an important first step in the investment decision-making process.

Taking the example shown in table 6.2 (see p. 69) a little further, let's imagine we required an annual return of only 4 or 5 per cent to reach our five-year goal for our $100 weekly investment. In that case it might have been wiser to have invested in cash and taken on less risk. Even though at the end of the five years we were able to sell the shares for $38 760, there was a high likelihood that at some stage during our period of ownership the shares dipped in value (for example, as a result of the GFC).

Liquidity

Liquidity refers to the ease of access to our funds. To liquidate our assets means to convert our assets back into cash. The level of liquidity relates to how quickly we could get our hands on the money, if we were to decide to liquidate our investment today.

Different investments have different levels of liquidity based on the way they are bought and sold and the market demand for these assets. Market demand refers to how many buyers there are at any point in time.

Cash in a bank account is highly liquid, whereas it might take us weeks, months or even years to find someone who is willing to pay a fair price for our diamond. Artworks or other collectables fall into the same category as this.

Shares are generally fairly liquid. The ASX provides a very easy platform for us to buy and sell our shares quickly and efficiently. However, if our investment was in a small company that many people have not heard of, this could affect the liquidity of the stock, because there might not be any willing buyers at the time we decide to sell.

Property can also take some time to sell, depending on market conditions. The other factor to take into consideration with property is the settlement period, which refers to the number of days after the property is sold before we receive our money and the property officially transfers into the name of the buyer. Settlement periods in Australia are commonly anywhere between 30 and 90 days.

The liquidity of an asset should form part of our decision-making process. For example, we should not invest money in illiquid assets if we are likely to need quick access to it. This is why sinking all our money into property as our first investment is not necessarily the smartest decision we can make. It's always important to keep some liquid investments, such as cash or shares, so we can access funds in the case of an emergency.

If we are forced to sell an illiquid asset quickly, we will often find we are unable to achieve fair value for it. Without the flexibility to wait for a better offer, we may need to accept the first one that comes along. Essentially, we have the lower hand when it comes to this type of transaction. With an illiquid asset, it is better to be able to wait for the right offer to come along.

Investment 101: asset classes

Now we understand the different characteristics we need to consider when evaluating an investment, it's time to delve a little deeper into the main assets we can use to build our wealth: these are cash (chapter 7), shares (chapter 8) and property (chapter 9). One other major, often overlooked asset is our own ability to work and produce an income, so in chapter 10 we'll also consider ways we can maximise our earnings potential in order to gain access to more money to invest and put to work for us. Part II winds up by reviewing the greatest savings vehicle of all—superannuation (chapter 11). All of these considerations will help to shape the goal-setting decisions arrived at in chapter 15.

Key points

→ Capital refers to the purchase price, sale price or current value of any investment we hold.

→ Income refers to the interest, rent or dividend payments received by the owner of an investment.

→ Not all investment will fluctuate in capital value, and not all investments will produce an income.

→ All investments bear some level of risk, usually related to the level of return possible.

→ Liquidity refers to how quickly we can realise the value of an investment—that is, sell it and receive cash.

Putting it into action

In the next chapters we will go into more detail about the common types of investment assets available. Before we start, use table 6.3 to create a list of types of investments you currently own, and what characteristics apply to each of those assets. Don't forget to look into any investments that are held within your superannuation fund.

Table 6.3: my current investments

Investment type	Characteristics	Ownership structure
1_____	_____	Personal/joint/super
2_____	_____	Personal/joint/super
3_____	_____	Personal/joint/super
4_____	_____	Personal/joint/super
5_____	_____	Personal/joint/super
6_____	_____	Personal/joint/super

While you read through the rest of part II, think about your current investments (including any cash) and whether or not they are appropriate for your needs. Think about what you are trying to achieve and whether or not the characteristics of each investment are likely to help you attain this.

CHAPTER 7

Investing
in
cash

A penny saved is a penny earned.

Benjamin Franklin

Cash is the simplest form of investment, and the one most of us are familiar with. Growing up in Melbourne, Australia, I had a Commonwealth Bank Dollarmite Savings Account, as many of us did. Each week my parents would send me off to school with 50 cents tucked into the plastic yellow folder that contained my deposit book. Each time I received my deposit book back, I would see my balance grow. I was encouraged from a young age to save for things I wanted.

The first thing I ever saved for was a bike: it was $74 and my parents agreed to pay half on the condition that I saved the other half. I was only about six years old and it must have taken me a long time to reach my goal, but every time I walked past that toy store I would look at my purple bike in the window. I kept watching my balance grow until finally one day we all went in together and bought my bike.

The bonus of interest

It was a great feeling and it taught me a good early lesson about saving and the pleasure of delayed gratification. As a teenager I moved on to an online savings account in order to save for bigger goals. I would divide the total amount I needed for an item by the number of weeks I had to save up for it, and come up with a weekly amount I needed to put into my savings account in order to reach my goal. The bonus was the interest I earned along the way, which helped me reach my savings goals just a little sooner.

How does it work? Essentially, when you deposit your money into a bank account, the bank is then able to use your money to lend to other customers. In turn, the customers who have borrowed money from the bank are charged an interest rate, usually each month, on the balance of the funds they have borrowed. If you jump onto any bank's website, you will see they offer many different savings products and loan products, all with varying interest rates. But you won't find an interest rate on a savings product that's higher than the rate being charged on a loan product, because this margin is where the banks make their money.

Loan products include credit cards, personal loans, car loans and, of course, mortgages. Generally, the bigger the loan, and the longer the repayment term, the lower the interest rate. The reverse applies to savings accounts, as we can see in table 7.1.

Table 7.1: common bank products and associated interest rates

Product	Common time frame	Example of interest rate
Everyday account	Less than 30 days	0%
Online savings account	Up to 1 year	5%
Term deposit	Up to 5 years	6%
Mortgage	25–30 years	7%
Personal loan	5–10 years	11%
Credit card	30–55 days	18%

Note that the above rates are examples only to give an idea of the relationship between the interest a bank will pay versus the interest a bank will charge. Interest rates vary all the time according to economic conditions. The Reserve Bank of Australia (RBA) is responsible for determining the monetary policy in Australia. The RBA sets the cash rate and aims to keep inflation low and stable. The board of the RBA meets on the first Tuesday of each month to make decisions regarding the cash rate. Any changes made to this rate will usually be reflected in the interest rates set by banks and financial institutions in the days following an RBA announcement.

Volatility and risk

Cash is considered a stable investment (with low volatility) characterised by a low level of risk. Although the interest rate we earn can vary depending on market conditions, we will usually have ample warning of any change and won't see the rate varying a huge amount in a short period of time.

Cash is also a highly liquid investment option. Using online savings accounts and everyday accounts, our money can usually be transferred instantly, or at least overnight. Even term deposits, which have a fixed agreed term, can be broken at any time to give us access to our funds (although there is usually a fee or interest penalty associated with doing this).

Invested in the right product (such as a term deposit or an online savings account), our cash will provide us with a reliable return on investment, based on current rates of interest, at very little risk.

There is, however, no capital growth associated with cash. A dollar invested today is still a dollar in 10 years' time, but today's dollar will buy us more than the same dollar will buy us in 10 years. (Remember when the most expensive ice creams were 95 cents? Today you need about $3.50 for the same treat.) This is called inflation and is the hidden 'expense' that will eat away at our cash over time.

The effects of inflation on cash

Let's assume we inherited $100000 and invested it in a five-year term deposit at a fixed interest rate of 6 per cent. We receive $6000 in income every year (which is taxed at our marginal tax rate). In the first year that income was enough to provide us with a great overseas holiday, but after five years we notice that we don't have enough for the same holiday any more, and we need either to stay in cheaper accommodation, go for a shorter period of time or use other money to make up the difference.

After the five years is up, our term deposit matures (which means we can access the money again), but unfortunately the $100000 we were going to use as a hefty home deposit is now worth only about $89 000 (and house prices have gone up in the meantime). Table 7.2 illustrates these effects over a five-year period.

Table 7.2: effects of inflation on cash investment

	Year 1	Year 2	Year 3	Year 4	Year 5
Term deposit	$100 000	$100 000	$100 000	$100 000	$100 000
Income (at 6%)	$6 000	$6 000	$6 000	$6 000	$6 000
Tax (at 31.5%)	−$1 890	−$1 890	−$1 890	−$1 3890	−$1 890
Net income	$4 110	$4 110	$4 110	$4 110	$4 110
Holiday cost*	−$4 110	−$4 233	−$4 360	−$4 491	−$4 625
Out of pocket	$0	−$123	−$250	−$381	−$515
Term deposit	$100 000	$100 000	$100 000	$100 3000	$100 000
Term deposit value*	$100 000	$97 087	$94 259	$91 514	$88 848

*Indexed/discounted by 3 per cent average inflation.

When we add up all of the income received (after removing the tax), and the fact that we still have $100 000 at the end of five years, we can conclude that the total investment return is $20 550. However, when we add up the term deposit's discounted value, plus the income (less tax and out-of-pocket costs), the real investment return is actually $8129.

This is not at all to suggest that cash is a bad investment. Cash is a great place for short-term savings and emergency funds and as part of a larger investment portfolio in order to offset other, more volatile investments. It is, however, important to consider the effect inflation will have on our investments, as on all other assets.

What if we didn't spend the income but left it in the bank to earn more interest? This is referred to as compound interest, which we discussed earlier. Let's have a look at it again, using our $100 000 term deposit as an example.

The power of compound interest

Let's say we apply the same scenario as above but instead of spending the income we simply leave it in the account to accumulate further interest. Tax would still need to be paid, but I have left it out of table 7.3 for the sake of clarity. Look at the income line here in comparison to the one in table 7.2.

Table 7.3: effect of compound interest on cash investment

	Year 1	Year 2	Year 3	Year 4	Year 5
Opening balance	$100 000	$106 000	$112 360	$119 102	$126 248
Income (at 6%)	$6 000	$6 360	$6 741	$7 146	$7 575
Closing balance	$106 000	$112 360	$119 102	$126 248	$133 823

There is still no capital growth (the dollars are still just dollars), and inflation would need to be taken into consideration, but we can again see the power of the interest received earning future interest and the compound effect this has.

The important characteristics to remember about investing in cash are:

- There will be no increase or decrease in capital value.
- Income is earned in the form of interest paid by the bank.
- It is a relatively low-risk investment option.
- The effects of inflation over the long term should be considered.

Table 7.4 summarises the advantages and disadvantages of investing in cash.

Table 7.4: the pros and cons of cash investment

Pros	Cons	Suited for
Highly liquid	No capital growth	Short-term savings goals
Low risk	Effects of inflation	Emergency funds
Stable income		

Ways to invest in cash

Table 7.5 provides examples of different ways we can invest in cash or cash-like investments.

Table 7.5: cash investment vehicles

Investment	Characteristics
Online savings account	*Risk:* very low *Liquidity:* high
Term deposit	*Risk:* very low *Liquidity:* high (with penalties)

Fixed interest

Another asset class worth mentioning is fixed interest. I have included it in this chapter as it has similar characteristics to cash; however, it functions a little differently. Fixed interest assets, commonly referred to as bonds, pay the owner regular interest for an agreed period of time. During this period of time, the underlying bond can be bought and sold at a value that is influenced by the interest rate payable on the bond in comparison to the current RBA cash rate. The biggest difference between cash and bonds is that the underlying value of a bond can fluctuate, whereas a dollar in the bank is always a dollar.

Table 7.6 provides examples of different ways we can invest in fixed interest investments.

Table 7.6: fixed interest investment vehicles

Investment	Characteristics
Managed funds	*Risk:* low to medium *Liquidity:* high
Government bonds	*Risk:* low *Liquidity:* medium
Corporate bonds	*Risk:* medium *Liquidity:* medium

A managed fund is an investment vehicle we can use to gain exposure to a broad range of different cash and fixed interest style investments. Different countries and institutions will offer different products at varying rates of interest. Managed funds have been developed so that investors can pool their money and allow a fund manager to select the best cash and bond products available, and monitor them on an ongoing basis.

Bonds are investments that carry similar characteristics to cash but essentially cut out the middle man (the bank). Instead of borrowing from a bank, a company can issue bonds that are made available to investors for purchase in return for a promised interest payment. Governments do the same. A government bond is considered fairly secure, whereas a corporate bond needs to be evaluated based on the stability of the company. The Australian bond market isn't as liquid or large as markets in other parts of the world, and currently accessing corporate and government bonds requires a substantial sum of money. This is changing, however, with companies turning increasingly to the retail market for funding as they rely less on the banks.

In summary, cash is a stable and secure investment option best suited to short-term savings goals, as an emergency fund or buffer account, or to provide stability in a larger investment portfolio. Fixed interest bonds are similar to cash in that they provide a regular interest payment over an agreed period of time. However, they often require a larger sum of money to buy in, making investing in fixed interest through managed funds more common.

Cash and fixed interest assets will generally not provide us with returns that are above the norm, and the often overlooked negative effects of inflation should always be considered.

Key points

→ Cash and cash-style investments are relatively low-risk and stable investment options.

→ Don't underestimate the negative effects of inflation on your cash.

→ Compound interest combined with time is a powerful combination.

Putting it into action

If you don't already use a high-interest online savings account, it's time to set one up today and start saving. If you already have some cash saved in a bank account, and it's not in a high-interest online savings account, you need to switch it pronto!

A great idea is to open an account with a banking institution other than the one you currently use, as this will make it slightly more difficult for you to access your money, reducing the temptation to dip into your savings account.

→ *Step 1.* Research the currently available options and interest rates, and select the most competitive.

→ *Step 2.* Establish a new account (generally you can do this quickly online).

→ *Step 3.* Establish a regular transfer into your savings account immediately after pay day. Ten per cent of your wages is a great place to start. When you arrive at your goal-setting decisions in chapter 15 you can make adjustments to this if required to meet your different savings goals.

How much should I save?

If you're wondering how much you should be aiming for, a great starting point is to build up an emergency fund or buffer account, equivalent to three months' salary. Table 7.7 will help you calculate this, based on what you receive each pay cycle.

Table 7.7: pay cycle savings calculation

Pay cycle	Savings amount
Weekly	$_____ x 13 = $_____
Fortnightly	$_____ x 6.5 = $_____
Monthly	$_____ x 3 = $_____

CHAPTER 8
Investing
in
shares

You only have to do a very few things in your
life so long as you don't do too many things wrong.

Warren Buffett

Shares are easier to understand than you might think, and although they can seem a little scary to a first-time investor, the reality is that most of us have been investing in shares for years without even realising it. This is because, unless we have selected otherwise, it is more than likely that our superannuation is invested in some form of managed fund that is invested in shares (along with cash and property).

In the previous chapter we looked at how any money we deposit with the bank is then lent out to people and companies, so when we put our money in the bank, we are essentially becoming a loaner. For example, a company borrows the money we deposit in the bank to invest in development that they hope will increase the value of the company. If they are willing to pay, for example, 7 per cent interest to the bank (where we are receiving just 5.5 per cent), then obviously they are expecting to produce a return greater than 7 per cent by using the bank's money (our money) to invest in the growth of the firm.

So why not become an owner of companies, instead of a loaner? That way we can benefit from both capital growth and income. Obviously, not all our money should be placed into shares, but investing in shares should certainly form part of any well-diversified wealth creation strategy.

How does it work? Essentially, when we buy shares we buy a small stake in the company. As a shareholder we are now a part-owner in the company whose shares we own. This ownership entitles us to a portion of the annual profits, which we receive as dividends, and if the company increases or decreases in value our shares will reflect this. Rather than making a dividend payment, a company might decide to retain the profits in order to invest in further growth and development. This is not necessarily a bad thing for shareholders as it would hopefully result in the share price increasing over time.

Share prices go up and down depending on how the company is viewed in the marketplace (by potential buyers). Interestingly, the current price of its shares does not always accurately reflect the actual value of the company.

Active versus passive investing

The term *active investing* refers to a style of investing in shares that ultimately revolves around trying to time the market — that is, seeking out shares believed to be undervalued with potential for growth, usually over the short term. To do this well requires a huge amount of research and information, along with a thorough knowledge of the sharemarket and how to evaluate a stock. It is possible, however, and many ordinary investors trade shares on the stock market on a regular basis using CommSec, E*TRADE or a similar online portal. These online services make it very easy to deposit cash and then to buy and sell shares quickly and efficiently at a low cost.

We can also actively invest over the longer term. This simply means deciding where we believe there are long-term opportunities for investment, making the decision to invest and then sticking with it. Because we have consciously made this decision instead of just putting our money in the market, this is still defined as active investing.

For those of us who do not wish to handle the investment decisions ourselves, we can still invest actively through the use of an active-style fund manager or investment adviser. All this means is that we believe it is possible to select shares that will outperform the average of the sharemarket, and we are entrusting to a professional the task of delivering these results.

Passive investing is often cheaper because the workload that comes with constant monitoring, evaluating and decision making is taken out of the equation. Passive investors commonly invest in a representation of an index. The ASX 200 is an index that tracks the average of the top 200 stocks listed on the ASX. There is an ETF (exchange-traded fund) that aims to replicate the performance of the ASX 200; the code for this ETF is STW. Many different indexes are used to measure the markets, including sector-specific indices such as the XHJ, which is the Australian Health Care index.

In the chart in figure 8.1, we can track both the STW (ASX 200) and the XHJ (Australian Health Care) indices over a five-year period. Both could be considered passive investment options. If, however, we decided to invest in health care over the ASX All Ordinaries index because we believed it to be a growth area, this would have been an active decision that would have seen us outperforming the average of the market.

Figure 8.1: tracking the STW and XHJ indices, 2003–12

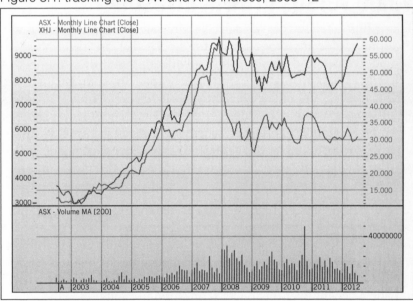

Looking at the chart, though, prior to year 4 we might have started questioning our decision, as the two indexes were tracking along a similar path. This is where investor behaviour plays such a big role in investing. Having a plan at the outset and sticking with it is what will lead us to wealth; chopping and changing generally doesn't pay off.

This is not to say active investing isn't a good idea, but rather that a decision needs to be made at the beginning of any investment period on whether to invest actively or passively, and then we should stick to that plan.

In a nutshell, an active investor believes it is possible to outperform the average of the market, whereas a passive investor does not. Generally, you take on slightly more risk as an active investor. Some believe that different market conditions call for different styles of investing, yet in a way this in itself represents an active approach because it advocates changing investment style depending on market conditions.

Value versus growth investing

Taking this a step further, we can compare value investing with growth investing. Value investors search for stocks that are determined to be undervalued and paying a high dividend, based on a number of different valuation models. Growth investors, by contrast, take the view that stocks are priced efficiently by the market. Growth investors are more concerned with evaluating the potential for growth in a stock based on economic trends than whether the stock is currently priced fairly. Growth investors will accept lower dividend payments when they know the company they own is reinvesting the profits in order to grow.

As you can imagine, a high income–producing stock would be more beneficial to a retiree investor who needs to live off the income. On the other hand, a young person who does not require income (in fact, who may even prefer to avoid generating income they would need to pay tax on) may be more inclined to look for growth stocks that will provide a benefit over the longer term through capital growth.

Volatility and risk

Shares are considered a volatile investment characterised by a medium to high level of risk. That said, some shares are much riskier than others and it is possible to establish a relatively conservative share portfolio. By investing in large, stable companies with a proven track record and a commitment to paying a regular dividend to shareholders, we can build a more predictable portfolio.

Shares are generally highly liquid in nature owing to constant market demand and excellent online facilities that allow trading to occur between 10 am and 4 pm each business day. We can benefit from this even when using managed funds or separately managed accounts to access shares, and can generally sell down our investments and access our funds within a number of days.

Starting small

One of the great things about share investing is that we can start small, either by investing in shares directly or through a managed fund or separately managed account. With as little as a few hundred dollars, we can open an online account using a platform such as CommSec or E*TRADE (there are several others), deposit some funds from our bank account and get started right away.

We can select a stock to purchase or simply invest in an index such as the ASX 200 using the stock code STW. This stock code purely replicates the investment performance of the ASX 200, which means we are able to access broad exposure cheaply and efficiently.

It's important to check the brokerage fees to ensure they are not too high per trade. Some online providers offer free brokerage for a period to get us started. We would want the brokerage fees to be as low as possible, because this is part of the cost of investing. For example, $15 in brokerage for a $100 placement (or 15 per cent brokerage) is too high; it would take a long time to recover that initial cost, reducing the overall return of the investment.

If we have a little more to get started with, there are many managed funds, separately managed accounts and exchange-traded funds that will generally cost less than 1 per cent in brokerage to get started or in ongoing management fees. If we have between $2000 and $5000 to get started, we will generally be able to open one of these accounts and can often invest as little as $250 each month through a direct debit arrangement.

Dollar cost averaging

Contributing to a share portfolio or managed fund regularly will generally provide us with the greatest return over a longer period of time. This approach, referred to as *dollar cost averaging*, means we buy into an investment regularly and at different prices. Instead of agonising over what day is the best day to invest in a particular share or fund, and at what price, we simply contribute the same regular amount of money and benefit from the fluctuations in price that occur over time.

If we think about it, when markets are down it means share prices are lower and essentially our investments are on sale. When this occurs, we get to buy more shares (or units in a managed fund) for our money. If we continue to contribute the same amount each month for many years, market fluctuations will add a huge amount of value to our portfolio. Why? Because we'll own many more shares than we would if we bought only when markets were up.

Most of us haven't felt too eager to buy shares over the past few years since the GFC, yet this period may represent the greatest fire sale we will ever see in our lives. If we'd been clever enough to keep investing each month over this period, imagine how many individual shares or units we might now own! So when markets rally again, we'd have more exposure to the upturn and would benefit as our share prices increased once again. In reality, such an approach goes against our emotional responses, and most of us continue to buy when the markets are high and to sell out and sit back when markets are low.

This is why it is important we have a plan, know why we are investing and what our time frame is, and stick to it, irrespective of what happens in investment markets. The price of our portfolio really matters only when we need to sell it, not along the way.

The important characteristics to remember about investing in shares are:

- the underlying value of a share can change (either up or down) over time
- shares will usually pay income to us in the form of a dividend, which is a portion of company profits

- shares are a medium to high risk investment option, depending on the stocks selected
- shares are generally highly liquid in nature.

Table 8.1 summarises the advantages and disadvantages of investing in shares.

Table 8.1: the pros and cons of investing in shares

Pros	Cons	Suited for
Highly liquid	Medium–high risk	Medium- to long-term savings goals
Capital growth	Too much choice	Building long-term wealth
Stable income		Income-producing asset for retirement

Ways to invest in shares

Table 8.2 provides examples of different ways we can invest in shares.

Table 8.2: share investment vehicles

Investment	Characteristics
Direct shares	*Risk:* medium–high *Liquidity:* high
Exchange traded funds	*Risk:* medium–high *Liquidity:* high
Separately managed accounts	*Risk:* medium–high *Liquidity:* high
Managed funds	*Risk:* medium–high *Liquidity:* medium–high

As we've discussed, an exchange-traded fund (ETF) provides us with a simple and cost-effective way to invest in a representation of a particular index, such as the ASX 200. ETFs are becoming increasingly popular as a cheap way to gain exposure to different investment markets, moving beyond sharemarkets alone to include almost anything you could imagine investing in.

A separately managed account (SMA) is essentially a portfolio of shares that the investor will own directly, although they are selected and managed by a fund manager. This is a great way to invest in a diversified share portfolio with less money, as you will achieve a great reduction in brokerage costs because these costs are split across a large pool of investors. You also retain ownership of the individual stocks and at any time can take over the management of the stocks yourself, choosing when to buy and sell. SMAs are relatively new to the Australian market and will, I believe, become more popular over time.

There are a huge number of managed funds available to Australian investors, with many, many different investment focuses (not just shares). Investors own units in the managed fund and the value of those units goes up and down; they don't own individual assets within the fund and often don't know exactly what assets are held each day. All funds will have a mandate they need to hold to. For example, the fund manager of an actively managed, large cap Australian equities fund might be required to invest in large Australian companies at all times, holding less than 5 per cent cash, and at all times to actively trade those shares in order to provide returns for shareholders. This way investors know the fund manager is always investing their money as they intended it to be invested.

In summary, shares will provide you with an investment that will grow in both capital value and income payments over the longer term. However, there is a higher level of risk associated with investing in shares as there is a possibility that the company we are invested in isn't successful, or even fails, in which case we could lose all our money. We can reduce this risk by investing in a diverse range of stocks.

Key points

→ Be an owner, not a loaner.

→ Owning shares means you own a portion of the company.

→ Active investors believe they can beat the market average; passive investors invest in the market generally, confident that ultimately it will trend upward.

→ The stock code STW replicates the average top 200 Australian companies (ASX 200).

→ Dollar cost averaging is a great way to buy into your investments regularly at different prices over time without the need to time the market.

Putting it into action

Establish your own watch list. A watch list is a list of shares you are interested in and are monitoring. The easiest way to do this is using an app on your smart phone. There are plenty available that allow you to create and select from a list of companies and at any time view the price of an individual company from this list. CommSec allows you to establish an account and set up watch lists before you have purchased any actual investments. This is a great place to start, as you can follow a couple of companies you are interested in and get a feel for their individual share prices and how the market moves.

Pick something you're interested in

Make a list of your favourite Australian companies and then visit the ASX website (www.asx.com.au) to see if they are listed on the exchange. If they are, you can obtain their three-letter stock code and enter it into your watch list. This way you'll stay a lot more focused and learn faster as you'll be following companies you're actually interested in.

Over time, you'll naturally start to broaden your interest to other companies and see the effects of different economic and non-economic events on company share prices and the ASX 200.

CHAPTER 9

Investing
in
property

*Experienced investors will tell you there's no ideal time
to buy an investment and, if there was, most people
only recognise it with hindsight.*

Annette Sampson

Most of us see property as a safe and easily understood investment vehicle. In Australia investing in property is widely considered a sign of success. Historically, property has provided excellent returns, and the fact that it is a physical asset that we can see, feel and touch appeals to many of us.

I purchased my first property at the age of 26 after saving a $50 000 deposit, and I admit that the main reason I did this was because of the social pressure I felt. It was a good property in a nice area and didn't require much maintenance. Unfortunately, when the relationship I was in broke down less than two years later, I was faced with the need to sell it long before I had intended.

This was a big lesson for me in the truth that property is a long-term investment, mainly because of the high costs associated with purchase, such as stamp duty and legal fees. Unless you're sure you will be keeping it for a long period of time, it's important to consider all your options before investing in a property.

At the time I had established a very small portfolio of managed funds with $1000 and was contributing a few hundred dollars each month to it. Maintaining this investment became quite difficult while I owned the property. Interest rates rose from 5 to 9 per cent in the first year, almost doubling the mortgage repayments I had to make. Somehow, thankfully, I managed to hold on to my portfolio.

After I sold the property for $35 000 more than I had paid for it, I calculated that I was actually down about $16 000 in the end, once interest, stamp duty and legal fees were taken into account. Of course, this wouldn't have been the case if I had held the property for 10 or more years, but circumstance forced me to sell.

A property we purchase to live in is defined as a principal residence. As we are occupying the property it will obviously not produce any income. In this instance, the property will likely provide capital growth over the long term but no income in the meantime. If we purchase an investment property, it will provide income while it is rented out to someone else and will also likely provide capital growth over the long term.

Capital gains tax

In Australia there are different tax treatments for an investment property and a principal residence. We pay no capital gains tax when selling a principal residence; we do pay capital gains tax on selling an investment property. The rental income received from an investment property is also taxable, although any interest expenses are deductible. Any repairs to the property are tax deductible in the year they occur, whereas improvements form part of the cost base. This means we won't get a tax deduction for them now, but they will be added to the cost base of the property when it is sold later (reducing the capital gains amount).

Capital gains tax is payable on any investment we hold and sell for an amount that is more than we purchased it for, including property and shares. The capital gain is the difference between what we paid for the investment and what we sold it for, and includes any costs incurred along the way that improved (or added value) to the asset. The capital gain is the amount we need to pay tax on in that income year.

If we hold the asset for less than 12 months, the entire capital gain amount forms part of our income and we will be taxed at our marginal rate. If we hold the asset for more than 12 months, the capital gain amount is discounted by 50 per cent, so we pay tax at our marginal rate on only half the capital gain amount.

Table 9.1 shows how the capital gains tax is calculated in two examples, based on the same figures, but with one property held for more than 12 months and the other held for less than 12 months.

Table 9.1: effects of capital gains tax on property

Property held over 12 months		Property held less than 12 months	
Purchase price	$500 000	Purchase price	$500 000
Stamp duty and costs	$26 500	Stamp duty and costs	$26 500
Renovations	$18 000	Renovations	$18 000
Cost base	$544 500	Cost base	$544 500
Sale price	$620 000	Sale price	$620 000
Capital gain	$75 500	Capital gain	$75 500
Assessable gain (50% disc.)	$37 750	Assessable gain (100%)	$75 500
Tax payable at 38.5% MTR	$14 534	Tax payable at 38.5% MTR	$29 068
Net profit	**$60 966**	**Net profit**	**$46 433**

Capital gains tax can be an important consideration when selling any investment asset. If it isn't going to make a lot of difference to the price we are able to achieve, and we have held the asset for less than 12 months, it may be worth holding it for the full year. That said, if there is a lot of fluctuation in price and a good offer is on the table, it may be smarter to dispose of the asset when the opportunity arises, rather than risking a much reduced offer.

Renovator's delight

Because of the high costs of acquiring property, it is generally a long-term investment. However, some people are able to generate a good living purely through buying rundown properties, renovating them and selling them on for a profit. This activity could be compared with an active day trader of the stock market who hunts for mispriced shares and aims to turn them around quickly for a profit. Just like day trading the stock market, short-term investment is a far riskier way to invest in property, but it can suit people with the right mix of market knowledge and practical skills.

Volatility and risk

Property is considered a more stable investment than shares, mainly because, as an unlisted asset, it is impossible to track the value of a property on a daily basis. If we were able to do this, we might be shocked by how volatile property really is. Imagine auctioning your home every single day!

Among the main risks associated with property are urgent, unexpected repairs and maintenance. Particularly if it is an investment property with tenants, we have no choice but to spend the money and fix any problems right away. Unfortunately, there is no return on additional costs incurred to ensure the property is kept to a minimum standard so our tenants will continue to pay rent. The other big risk associated with an investment property is vacancy. For every week we do not have a tenant in our property, the annual rental income is reduced, along with the effectiveness of the investment and the overall return.

Additional risks include flood, fire or serious damage caused by a tenant. There are insurance policies to cover these expenses, although it is important to factor the insurance premiums into the cost of owning the property.

Property is a relatively illiquid investment option, mainly because of the time required to find a buyer once we have made the decision to sell, and the settlement period following the sale. This is not a huge concern, provided we have ready access to other funds, but it is a factor that should be considered before purchasing a property.

The important characteristics to remember about investing in property include the following:

- Property is generally a longer term investment because of the costs associated with purchase.
- Income is derived from rent, and interest payments are tax deductible if the property is an investment.

- Capital gains tax needs to be paid on sale but does not apply to a principal residence.
- Property is fairly illiquid, so ensure you have ready access to cash.

Table 9.2 summarises the advantages and disadvantages of investing in cash.

Table 9.2: the pros and cons of property investment

Pros	Cons	Suited for
Tangible asset	Highly illiquid	Long-term savings goals, such as retirement
Stable income	Costly to purchase	
Capital growth	Unexpected costs	Purchasing a home to live in

Ways to invest in property

We can access property as an investment in a number of different ways, not just through purchasing directly ourselves. Table 9.3 provides examples of different ways we can invest in property, some of which we can do using far less capital, while passing on the management costs and ownership headaches to a professional fund manager.

Table 9.3: property investment vehicles

Investment	Characteristics
Direct property	*Risk:* medium–high *Liquidity:* low
Managed funds	*Risk:* medium–high *Liquidity:* medium
Listed property trusts	*Risk:* medium–high *Liquidity:* medium

Most of us will spend some time determining our buying criteria and researching our chosen area before purchasing a property directly (through auction or private sale). Alternatively, it is possible to use a buyer's agent, who is a professional property expert who will research the property market for us and, based on the criteria established, make recommendations. Many of these agents will handle the bidding and offer process too.

We can also invest in property through managed funds or listed property trusts; many of us have some exposure automatically to these from within our superannuation funds. Similar to a managed fund that invests in shares, a listed property trust is an investment vehicle that we can use to gain broad exposure to a range of property — commonly commercial or large residential developments. For someone with a strong belief in property but who feels uncomfortable with the high cost barriers to entry, a managed fund or listed property trust can be a great way to begin investing in property.

The only way is up

History shows us that all investments ultimately trend upwards, even though it doesn't always feel that way. The media are full of doomsday stories because they sell more papers than tales of 'another good day for investment markets'. Headlines such as 'Blood on the Floor on Wall Street!' sound far more exciting. It's no wonder we have all become so nervous about taking the plunge!

The important thing to remember is that we don't have to dive in head first; we can simply dip our toe in the water. We can build up a little cash, open a small share portfolio or managed fund, and once we've managed to move into a comfortable position, and have become used to putting money aside regularly, we can apply for a loan and buy a property.

The best way to learn about investments, other than reading books like this, is to start investing ourselves. Even though it is scary, we just need to start small and build up little by little, knowing that the odds over the long term are in our favour. Figure 9.1 shows the value of

$10 000 invested in 1980. Even with market ups and downs, investing that $10 000 instead of spending it or sticking it under the bed would have had a huge impact over time.

Figure 9.1: chart showing progress of investment vehicles over time

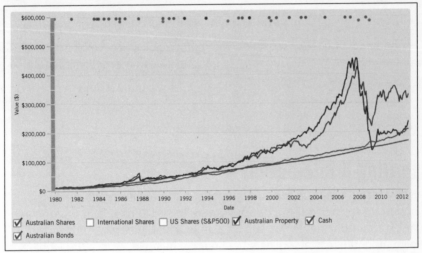

Source: Vanguard Investments Australia Ltd. Past performance is not an indicator of future performance. The chart shows the growth of $10 000 invested at the start of the selected period in an index representing the relevant asset class. The calculations contained within the chart are based on a set of assumptions. You should refer to the 'Assumptions' link attached to the Vanguard Interactive Index Calculator located at www.vanguard.com.au to view these assumptions. The results in the chart would be different if different assumptions were used. The information contained within the chart is intended for general informational purposes only. It is not intended as investment advice and must not be relied upon as such. Vanguard accepts no responsibility for any inaccuracies or omissions in the data or any reliance upon the information contained in the chart.

In summary, property can be a great long-term investment and contribute substantially to our overall wealth creation strategy. The most important things to consider when investing in property are the investment time frame, the costs associated with the purchase, and ensuring there is plenty of cash flow to cover the ongoing mortgage repayments and maintenance costs.

Key points

→ Your principal residence, the property you live in, is not subject to capital gains tax when sold.

→ Capital gains tax is payable on the sale of an investment property.

→ Because of costs associated with purchase and potential ongoing maintenance costs, property is generally a long-term investment.

→ Property is generally an illiquid asset, as it can take time to sell and settle on a property.

→ A 20 per cent deposit is a great place to start.

Putting it into action

If you haven't yet purchased a property, but are thinking about it, it's important to consider the deposit you will need to save and the ongoing mortgage repayments you will be able to afford. Visit www.infochoice. com.au and use their online calculators to help you determine what these costs might be.

Work out the maximum amount you are willing to spend (don't forget to factor in stamp duty), and calculate what 20 per cent of that is. This can become your savings goal. Ideally, you shouldn't look to purchase a property until you have this amount saved up in a high-interest savings account.

CHAPTER 10

Investing
in
you

An investment in knowledge pays the best interest.

Benjamin Franklin

One thing we can all do to increase our wealth is to increase our earning capacity. We can do this in a number of ways, and it is likely to occur of its own accord over time anyway, but the biggest problem we all have is that as we increase our earning capacity, we increase our spending capacity too!

For any increase in earnings to have a positive effect on our personal wealth creation, we need to continue to live as though our income has not increased, and to apply the increase to our savings and investments. If we do this, we will experience an exponential improvement in our capacity to build our wealth and to reach our goals and dreams.

Let's explore the different ways we may be able to increase our income.

Invest in knowledge

Upskilling or increasing our education levels can lead to a better job or a promotion or pay rise, based on our increased capacity to handle responsibility and a greater workload, or even a move into management. Sometimes we need to spend money to create money, and this could be one of those times. Perhaps it would be worthwhile approaching your employer about funding further training or education for you.

Many companies who see the organisational benefits of such training allocate a budget to employee development and education.

If you own your own business, there may be opportunities to explore new areas of service or production, or to charge a little more as your expertise increases.

Education and training costs are generally tax deductible (either to you individually, or to your business) if they are related to your field of work. Before enrolling in your chosen course check with your accountant or financial adviser, who should be able to help you with this. You may find your textbooks and associated expenses are also tax deductible.

Ask for a pay increase

If it is some time since you've received a pay increase, perhaps you should approach your boss or manager about this. It's important to remember that we're not automatically entitled to a pay rise just because we'd like one. Your employer invests in you by paying you a salary and expects a return on that investment.

Review your original job description and if you feel you have taken on more than was initially expected of you, or if you are exceeding your performance targets or expectations, take evidence of this to your boss to help explain why you deserve a pay rise. This may also be an opportunity to ask for greater responsibility, which will lead to your ongoing development and ultimately your continued promotion and increased earning capacity.

Review your pricing model

If you are a business owner, be sure to review your pricing model at least annually. Small business owners are notorious for unintentionally ripping themselves off by delivering high-quality products or services while charging too little. We often forget to review our pricing models and to increase prices with inflation or simply in line with fair value. Review your competitors, but also review your own costs and be sure you are charging appropriately.

As your business grows and you place larger orders or utilise more services, you may also need to renegotiate with suppliers. It's a good idea to review this annually too, as it may mean your costs can come down and you won't need to charge your customers more; instead, you'll just be able to benefit from the increased profit margin.

Start a business

The big disclaimer on this is that quitting your job and starting your own business is highly unlikely to lead you to produce more income in the short term! However, you may be able to start a little consulting or freelancing on the side to generate extra income without affecting your ability to perform your current role. If this proves lucrative, you may find yourself one day owning your own business.

Despite the common perception that sports and entertainment stars are among the world's wealthiest, more than 90 per cent of the *BRW* rich list have made their money through business. Once you have set yourself up financially, you may find that a short-term sacrifice in income while building a business will pay off over the long term. Starting a business is not for everyone, though, and certainly involves a high level of risk.

Get a second job

A safer option is to get a second job—a part-time job on the weekends or a couple of evenings a week, even for just a year. This could provide you with the increase in income you need to repay debt or to get ahead with your savings.

Sell stuff

Most of us have a truckload of possessions we don't need or use any more. Set up an eBay account and make money selling some of your old stuff. Although this won't turn you into a millionaire, if there's money to be made by selling some of our old junk, then why not? You'll feel good about it and generate a little extra income to put towards debt or to start savings while at the same time clearing out the clutter.

Follow your passion

I have noticed that those who follow their dreams will usually find that the money will follow them. The main reason for this is that it is a lot easier to work hard, and passionately, on something we love doing. So ask yourself: are you truly following your dreams and working in a career you love?

Not only will this make you happier, but you will have far more energy and creativity for the things you care about. If you're not in this situation, it may seem too hard to make a change, but if you can start by taking baby steps in the direction of the career you want, eventually you will find yourself where you want to be. Never ever give up on your dreams.

What about tax?

Now we're earning more, we need to consider the effect of tax on that extra income. Many of us assume it won't be worth earning more because we'll just be taxed more. This is partly true: we will have to pay tax on the additional income we earn, but we are only ever taxed incrementally and on a portion of our income, so it's always better to earn more.

In Australia, our tax rates are scaled — that is, we don't pay a flat rate of tax on all our income; we pay it in brackets. Essentially this means we needn't worry about having to pay a higher tax rate if we earn more, because we pay more tax only on the extra income. Table 10.1 shows the tax brackets for the 2012–13 tax year.

Table 10.1: tax brackets, 2012–13

Income	Tax payable
$0–$18 200	Nil
$18 201–$37 000	$0 plus 19% of any income between $18 201 and $37 000
$37 001–$80 000	$3572 plus 32.5% of any income between $37 001 and $80 000
$80 000–$180 000	$17 547 plus 37% of any income between $80 001 and $180 000
Over $180 000	$54 547 plus 45% of any income over $180 000

To find out how much tax you will need to pay on your expected gross income, www.taxcalc.com.au will calculate your tax payable in an instant. It will also calculate the Medicare levy, which is 1.5 per cent of your total income in addition to the tax rate.

The great tax return debate

A widely held misconception about personal taxation is that we should always receive a tax return. This usually begins because we received tax returns as young casual workers owing to the low-income tax offset. The low-income tax offset is currently $445 and is payable in full to anyone earning less than $37 000, after which it is reduced as our income increases until it is phased out completely.

The reality is that we will receive a tax return only if we have paid too much tax to the Australian Taxation Office (ATO) throughout the year. If we haven't paid enough, we may even have to pay tax to them after filing our annual tax return. Perhaps if instead we called it an annual tax reconciliation, its significance would be a little clearer.

Ideally, we have paid just enough tax to the ATO during the year that our return breaks even, as this means we will have had full access to our own money throughout the year—and ideally we have invested it! When we have money tied up with the ATO we do not receive any interest payments, so it's not ideal to overpay our tax, even though it's nice to get a return once a year.

Preparing in advance

To maximise your deductions and ensure you claim everything you are entitled to, I suggest meeting with a qualified accountant at the start of a new financial year, at the start of your career and at the start of a new job. Rather than waiting until the financial year is over, it's a lot better to find out in advance what you can and can't claim, as well as the best way to structure your investments and to make any new purchases.

Decisions on taking advantage of salary sacrifice options, saving receipts for items claimable related to your profession and purchasing investments in the best structure are very hard to undo or go back on once the time has passed, so it's always better to prepare in advance.

Salary sacrifice

This means paying for an expense with your pre-tax income. Depending on your current income, it could save you up to 46.5 per cent on purchases. Common items that can be salary sacrificed are laptops, superannuation payments and car leases, but what is allowed will depend on your occupation, ATO allowances and your employer. This is why it's important to work with a professional accountant or financial adviser who can provide informed advice in advance.

You are the reason to love your money

Many of us don't love money. Of course it's not really socially acceptable to admit to a love of money, as commonly this is perceived as materialistic or shallow. However, I believe it is time we all start to love our money. Why? Because, as we have discussed in this part of the book, our money is a direct reflection of what we do, because we earn money in return for what we put into the world. If we don't love our money, it could be argued that we're not really respecting ourselves and what it took for us to earn that money.

If we can start to think of our money as a direct reflection of our contribution to society, we may learn to feel differently about it—prouder, stronger and happier to have it and to treat it with respect. This mindset also makes it easier to assess whether or not we are receiving fair value for the work we do.

In the next chapter we'll take a closer look at what for most of us is the most important savings vehicle of all—superannuation.

Key points

→ Finding ways to increase your income is just as important as saving and investment.

→ There are many ways to increase your income, from starting a business on the side to selling possessions you no longer need.

→ It is always worth earning more money, even if you need to pay tax, as tax is paid on only a portion of each dollar you earn.

→ You will receive a tax return only if you have paid too much tax throughout the year.

Putting it into action

Selling things we no longer need is something all of us can do. Visit every room in your house, open the cupboards and drawers, and list all the items you no longer really need. Establish an eBay account and list these items for sale, specifying 'pickup only' for larger items to save yourself the time of dropping things off. Put any money you make directly into your high-income savings account, as this is all bonus money that you wouldn't otherwise have had. Your savings will grow before you know it, helping you reach your goals faster.

CHAPTER 11

Don't forget **about** retirement

It is always wise to look ahead, but difficult to look
further than you can see.

Winston Churchill

Retirement may feel a long way off, and not something worth dwelling on too much at the moment. Often we're having enough trouble meeting our current financial commitments, let alone thinking about whether or not we'll have adequate savings to fund a comfortable retirement.

We are lucky in Australia to have compulsory superannuation, which essentially forces us to save for retirement. Sadly, however, there is so little public education about what superannuation actually is that many of us either miss out on the opportunity altogether or leave it too late to take proper advantage of it. Superannuation is the greatest savings vehicle available to us. We just need to understand it better.

The other thing about superannuation is that almost all of us have it. If we earn more than $450 a month from employment, it is compulsory that our employer make superannuation contributions on our behalf. So why wouldn't we want to learn more about it? It's our money, and one day we'll use it to fund our retirement, so it's actually pretty important.

The earlier we start thinking about our retirement, the easier it will be to manage and plan. Unfortunately, I see many clients for the first time in their fifties, when they have finally realised that they may not have enough saved for their retirement, or that their assets are held in their personal names and they're facing serious tax implications when they do retire.

It's important to understand that our superannuation contributions, including the compulsory 9 per cent of our income contributed each year by our employers, will alone generally not be enough to provide for the retirement we would like. In almost all cases, we'll need to make additional contributions at some stage in order reach our retirement goals. The earlier we can think about this, the better.

Superannuation 101: what is it?

The most important thing you need to know about superannuation is that it is not an investment. We have discussed the different types of investments commonly available to us, and superannuation is not one of them. Rather, superannuation is a tax structure that is treated as a separate legal entity for tax purposes and is subject to different tax rates than individuals. It is a form of trust, with a trustee whose sole purpose is to ensure that the money contributed to the fund is invested appropriately to provide for the fund member's retirement.

Grasping this concept leads on to the realisation that we can choose what we invest in, in order to maximise our wealth for retirement. There are different funds available in the Australian marketplace, from very basic products with four or five investment options, right through to a self managed superannuation fund, which gives us the flexibility to invest in almost anything.

So if you thought you had never invested in anything other than cash savings in a bank account, the chances are you'd be wrong. Your superannuation is likely invested in a managed fund comprising cash, fixed interest, shares and property; you probably simply hadn't paid it much attention until now. But our superannuation is just as much our wealth as the money in our bank account, so we shouldn't just let it sit there. We need to take control of it, ensure we understand what we are invested in, and start thinking about whether it will provide us with enough for our retirement.

Types of funds

There are four main types of superannuation funds that offer varying degrees of flexibility and investment choice.

Basic industry funds

These funds offer only a small number of investments options (usually between four and seven). They are all managed funds that will be identified as 'conservative', 'balanced', 'growth', 'high-growth' or the like. They are often industry specific, charge relatively low fees and in return provide very little in the way of investment choice.

Standard industry or retail funds

These funds offer a selection of default fund options, with perhaps thirty or so other managed fund options included. Often people elect to put the bulk of their superannuation in one of the main investment options, such as a growth fund, and then pick a couple of other specific funds they are interested in for a small portion of their savings. Some industry funds and many retail funds operate in this way.

Comprehensive retail funds

This type of fund (almost always a retail fund, although some industry funds come close to it) allows us to investment in hundreds of different managed funds, the top 200 or even 300 Australian shares, separately managed accounts, term deposits and more. They provide a lot of flexibility, particularly as your account balance grows, and generally cost more. The guidance of a professional financial or investment adviser is often useful here.

Self managed superannuation funds

The last type of fund, which is growing in popularity, is the self managed superannuation fund (SMSF). An SMSF is a fund we establish ourselves (usually with the help of a lawyer, an accountant, an auditor and a financial or investment adviser). It provides us with the flexibility to invest in almost anything, provided it complies with the law. There are many laws governing SMSFs, and as the trustee of our own fund we are wholly and solely responsible for its management and compliance. If we do not abide by the law, hefty penalties and even jail time can result. Despite the 'self managed' tag, most people rely on the assistance of professionals to ensure their fund is operating appropriately. SMSFs generally become cost effective for those with balances above $300 000 and are not the best option until this level of wealth is reached, because of the fees associated with the establishment and ongoing maintenance of the fund.

We get what we pay for

Broadly speaking, with super funds we get what we pay for. It is important to consider the fees we are being charged in return for the investment options, reporting facilities and administration functions of the fund we select. In a very general sense, it is appropriate for a young person just starting to receive superannuation to be in one of the first options. As their balance grows they may wish to take more control, perhaps moving to the second option, and once they have reached $200 000 to $300 000 they may decide to move into a sophisticated retail fund or an SMSF. That said, many people elect to stay with the same basic industry fund their whole working life, and there is nothing to say the investment performance of their chosen option won't serve them well.

Irrespective of which fund we choose, it is important to assess and review the investment options we select either through our own research or with the help of a professional investment adviser. The money in our superannuation fund is an important part of our wealth accumulation strategy just like any other money. Investing it unwisely could make a huge difference to our ultimate retirement balance.

Tax benefits

As mentioned, superannuation is simply a tax structure that provides a highly beneficial environment in which to accumulate wealth. We discussed personal tax rates earlier in the book, and they can certainly be a little complicated, but we know that basically the more we earn, the more tax we need to pay on those additional earnings because we will move into a higher tax bracket. Superannuation tax is far simpler.

Our super fund is subject to a flat tax rate of 15 per cent payable on contributions and on any investment income earned (such as share dividends, bank interest or rental income from property). Table 11.1 shows how the money our employers put into our funds is treated.

Table 11.1: superannuation tax

Source	$	Based on
Annual salary	$100 000	
Superannuation guarantee (SG)	$9 000	9% of annual salary
Tax payable on SG	–$1 350	15% of superannuation guarantee
Net contribution to fund	$7 650	Superannuation guarantee less tax

As the tax rate within super remains flat at 15 per cent, it is unaffected by how much wealth we accumulate within our superannuation fund and how much income the investments are generating. Unlike investment income earned in our own name, which is subject to our marginal tax rate, we will always pay a maximum of 15 per cent in tax. Table 11.2 shows how the investment income inside the fund is taxed.

Table 11.2: tax on investment income within superannuation

Source	$	Based on
Superannuation balance	$85 000	
Investment income received	$3 720	Dividends, interest and so on
Tax payable on income	–$558	15% of income received
Superannuation balance	$88 162	Superannuation balance after income and tax

Did someone say tax-free?

The greatest tax benefits come into play later, however, when we retire. Currently, once we are over the age of 55 we can convert our superannuation into *pension phase*. We pay no tax at all on any investment income in pension phase. When we are in pension phase, we must draw an annual income, which is taxed between the ages of 55 and 60 but becomes completely tax-free from the age of 60. This is the power of holding assets within superannuation.

Don't plan too late!

As you can see, there is much to be said for directing all our investments into superannuation until the time we retire, as there will be no tax to pay on the income generated. The problem is, most people leave retirement planning until too late and are unable to transfer their assets in time. This is because there are limits on how much you can contribute into superannuation each year.

This is probably the biggest problem I have faced over the years with my wealthy older clients. They have led successful lives and built up substantial assets, but because of poor advice and lack of superannuation education, they have very little within their superannuation funds compared with the wealth they have created in their personal names, all of which is of course generating income that is taxable at their personal marginal tax rate — for the rest of their lives.

Superannuation contributions

Our employer is required by law to make a superannuation contribution of 9 per cent — that is, to deposit 9 per cent of our gross salary into our superannuation fund at least quarterly. We can make additional contributions or deposits into our fund in order to save more for our retirement. Two types of contributions can be used to build our retirement savings: these are referred to as concessional contributions and non-concessional contributions, and a different tax treatment is applied to each.

Concessional contributions are made with pre-tax dollars — money taken from your salary prior to tax being taken out. The two most common types of concessional contributions are the 9 per cent superannuation guarantee (SG) payment by your employer and salary sacrifice. Each year there is a limit (currently $25 000) on how much of this type of contribution we can make. By salary sacrificing we reduce our gross salary by the amount we have elected to contribute, thereby reducing the tax otherwise payable at our marginal tax rate.

Non-concessional contributions are contributions made to the fund with money that has already been taxed—money we have received from employment or investment earnings on which we have already paid tax. This type of contribution is not taxed at all when deposited into superannuation as it has already been taxed at our marginal tax rate. We can make an annual maximum of $150 000 of this type of contribution.

These annual limits seem high when we have only just begun our journey towards financial freedom. Many years down the track, though, when we have built substantial wealth and are starting to consider our retirement plans and to move our money into the tax-friendly superannuation environment, these limits can suddenly become quite restrictive. So the earlier we start, the better off we will be.

Limitations of superannuation

The biggest limitation of superannuation is that we cannot just withdraw money whenever we please—not, anyhow, until we reach a defined retirement age (referred to as *preservation age*, currently at least 55, depending on when you were born). It is therefore a balancing act to determine how much to put away now to increase our retirement savings later, while still being able to build up wealth that can be used to meet current and future lifestyle needs before we reach preservation age. It wouldn't be a good idea for a 20-year-old to salary sacrifice half of their salary into superannuation, for example, as they will likely need their savings sooner than 45 years down the track. That said, we will see in the example in the next section how a little increase in contributions earlier in life can save us having to play a precarious game of catch-up later.

Increasing your retirement savings

Now we have a pretty good understanding of the basics of superannuation and why it is a worthwhile vehicle through which we can and should accumulate wealth. There are a couple of strategies we can use to increase our retirement savings, and we'll be able to determine which one is most suited to us when we get to the goal-setting section later in the book.

Government co-contribution

The first strategy that every young person, part-time worker or low-income earner should consider taking advantage of is the *government co-contribution*. If we are working and earn an income from employment that is below $46 920, we are eligible for a part contribution; if we earn below $31 920 we are eligible for the full contribution.

How does it work?

If we make a non-concessional contribution (from tax-paid money) of up to $1000, the government will match it with 50 cents for every dollar we have contributed up to a maximum of $500. Given that many people will earn a lower salary for only a short period of their lives, taking advantage of this strategy while we can is important.

As an example, if we managed to make this $1000 contribution for three years in a row while at university between the ages of, say, 19 and 21, we would add $4500 to our retirement savings before we've even begun full-time employment ($3000 ourselves and $1500 from the government). The value of this $4500, invested over 45 years, is $143 000 (using an 8 per cent annualised return). Remember the power of compound interest.

How can we do this?

It seems hard to imagine being able to spare $1000 when we're studying, although it could be a great gift from a parent who wants to give their offspring a head start! I have also seen several diligent savers do this as young adults once they have understood there is really no other investment that will give you a 50 per cent return immediately, as this does. If you do want to do it yourself, most funds will allow you to establish a regular BPAY contribution into your fund. This equates to just $19.25 a week, or $83.30 a month.

Salary sacrifice

The second strategy that anyone who is working and earning income should consider is *salary sacrifice*, by which we forgo part of our pre-tax salary in order to make a contribution into our superannuation fund.

How does it work?

For anyone who earns above about $45 000 annually, which is roughly the crossover point when we start paying more than 15 per cent in tax on our income), this is worth considering. By salary sacrificing some of our income into superannuation, we are immediately gaining any of the tax payable on our money that would otherwise have been paid in tax over and above the rate of 15 per cent, although of course this is within our superannuation fund, not in our hand. Again, though, if we look at this as an investment return it's hard to beat, and there is no investment risk.

It's important first to determine how much we actually need in retirement and to work back from there. The following two tables illustrate the huge advantage of starting our contributions early. Table 11.3 shows approximately how much we would need to contribute on an annual, monthly or weekly basis, based on our current age, if our goal is to reach $1 000 000 at age 65 within superannuation (this includes your 9 per cent SG payments). Table 11.4 shows the same calculations for a goal of $2 000 000.

Table 11.3: target of $1 000 000 in super at age 65

Age	20	25	30	35	40	45	50	55	60
Annual	$1902	$2960	$4636	$7336	$11 806	$19 546	$34 059	$65 820	$167 092
Monthly	$158	$247	$386	$611	$984	$1 629	$2 838	$5 485	$13 924
Weekly	$37	$57	$89	$141	$227	$376	$655	$1 266	$3 213

Table 11.4: target of $2 000 000 in super at age 65

Age	20	25	30	35	40	45	50	55	60
Annual	$3803	$5919	$9272	$14 673	$23 613	$39 093	$68 118	$131 640	$334 185
Monthly	$317	$493	$773	$1 223	$1 968	$3 258	$5 676	$10 970	$27 849
Weekly	$73	$114	$178	$282	$454	$752	$1 310	$2 532	$6 427

As you can see, the longer we wait to start building our retirement savings, the more we will need to make up for. Luckily we all receive the 9 per cent superannuation guarantee, which gives us a head start, but planning ahead can mean a small impact on our lifestyle now translates into much greater rewards in the future.

MoneySmart (www.moneysmart.gov.au) has an excellent calculator tool you can use to track your superannuation and the impact salary sacrifice contributions will make.

How can we do this?

Once we have determined the additional contributions we would like to make to our superannuation, usually our employers will facilitate this. Speak with the HR or payroll department and ask them if they can arrange it. If you are self-employed, using the superannuation BPAY facility is usually the easiest way to make your regular superannuation payments. Often funds will have slightly different codes depending on the type of contribution you make, so be sure to check this out before establishing a regular automatic payment.

Remember, you can make up to $25000 annually in concessional contributions, which includes both employer SG contributions and salary sacrifice. If you accidentally contribute above this limit, you will incur a tax penalty at the highest marginal tax rate (currently 45 per cent). Anything above $25000 also counts towards your non-concessional contribution limit of $150000.

Non-concessional contributions

The next strategy to consider around the mid point of our working life (perhaps at age 40–45) is beginning to move the wealth we've already accumulated into superannuation via a *non-concessional contribution* strategy. At this age we are closer to reaching preservation age, when our superannuation becomes available to us, so there's less risk in our locking money away. All the assets we own that are held outside of superannuation will be generating income that is taxable at our highest marginal tax rate. Once we move this wealth into superannuation the income will be taxed at only 15 per cent, and then not at all in pension phase (currently over 55). We can see the importance over the long term of doing this, but the difficulty is moving our wealth across within a limited time frame.

How does it work?

Any non-concessional contributions we make into superannuation are not taxable on entry to the fund. This means if we put $50 000 into the fund, the full $50 000 can be invested according to our investment strategy.

How can we do this?

Any cash we have in the bank is easy, as there is no capital gains tax to pay. As we discussed earlier, cash does not increase in capital value—a dollar is always worth a dollar—so this is an easy and logical asset to move into superannuation. It's always important to keep a buffer or emergency account; however, if we have large sums of money in a bank account, making annual superannuation contributions of up to $150 000 will result in a lower tax rate on interest income earned going forward.

When it comes to shares, many funds will accept what is referred to as an *in specie transfer*. This means the shares don't need to be sold; they simply transfer ownership. When this occurs, capital gains tax is payable (if a capital gain has been made, of course) by us personally, as we have technically sold the shares to another entity. We can of course also sell the shares, contribute the cash into superannuation and then buy new investments within superannuation once the money has been received by our fund. In this case it would be worth determining which shares we want to sell and going from there. A professional investment adviser will be able to provide guidance on the best way to transfer or sell shares and boost our superannuation balance.

In relation to property, we are not permitted to make an in specie transfer of property into superannuation (except in the case of commercial property). We would be required to sell the property, pay any capital gains tax and then make a contribution into superannuation. Unless we planned to sell the property at that time, this is likely not the best solution, and it would be worth seeking professional advice before making this decision.

The bring-forward rule

There is one other important factor to note about non-concessional contributions, and that is the *bring-forward rule*. By law, we may at any time bring forward three years' worth of non-concessional contributions in order to make a lump-sum contribution of up to $450 000. If we decide to use this strategy to move a larger portion of wealth into the superannuation environment earlier, we need to keep in mind that we will not be able to make another non-concessional contribution until the fourth year, as we have used up the next three years' worth of non-concessional contributions.

If you are just beginning your wealth creation journey, this may seem to be of little relevance to you, but the more you understand now, the better equipped you will be for the future. Ideally, you will never need to maximise these transfer limits or use the bring-forward rule, because you have progressively built and managed your wealth effectively.

As we can see, superannuation is a very important part of our overall wealth creation journey, and the earlier we can start paying attention to it, the better off we will be in the long term. When you really think about it, we spend our life working in order to build enough wealth to one day retire, and the sooner we can achieve financial freedom, the better. Even if we don't stop working, and many people enjoy it so much they happily put off retirement, being able to *choose* to work, instead of having to, is an option most of us would like to have.

Now we have a better understanding of how different investments work, and why we need to start our personal journey to financial freedom sooner rather than later, we're ready to move on to part III. The following two chapters explore the psychology behind our financial behaviour and decision making. In chapter 14 we complete a budget and financial position assessment, so that in chapter 15 we are ready to set our specific financial goals. Chapter 16 underlines the vital importance of putting in place a good insurance plan. The final chapter advances the value of drawing on the knowledge of financial professionals and the experiences of friends during your journey.

Key points

→ Superannuation is a tax-effective environment, not an investment in itself.

→ You pay a flat tax rate of 15 per cent on income and no tax at all once retired and in pension phase.

→ You can invest in almost anything, including cash, term deposits, shares and property.

→ Check the fee you are paying, but remember that fees aren't everything and you generally get what you pay for.

→ The earlier you start building your retirement savings, the easier it will be.

Putting it into action

Get your funds in order

Many of us end up with more than one superannuation fund, usually because we have had a number of different part-time jobs before settling into our career. If this is you, it's time to arrange for them to be rolled over into a single fund.

Collect any of the past superannuation statements you can find so you have access to all the information for each of your funds. You may also wish to check the ATO Super Seeker website (https://superseeker.super. ato.gov.au) to search for any lost funds you may have.

You'll then need choose a fund (either one you already have or a new one) and apply to have all of your superannuation rolled into it. Before making your selection, consider the available investment options, online access capability, fees, services and member benefits.

It's a good idea to use the ATO's standard super rollover request form, which all funds must accept, and you will also need a certified copy of your driver's licence or another acceptable from of identification.

Don't forget to make sure your current employer is contributing into the fund you have selected.

Choose your investments

Once you have consolidated your superannuation into one account, it's time to have a look at what you're actually invested in and start taking control. All funds will have their own forms through which you can elect the investments you would prefer, and some will even allow you to do this online.

Don't forget to think about your time frame and what level of risk you are willing to take on in order to maximise your superannuation over the time you have left between now and retirement.

Ask your adviser

A financial adviser will be able to help you with all these steps, so if you already have one it's a good idea to chat with them first before doing the leg work yourself.

PART III

Now ... let's **get** going!

CHAPTER 12

Psychology **of** money

I will tell you how to become rich. Close the doors. Be fearful when others are greedy. Be greedy when others are fearful.

Warren Buffett

How we feel about money is shaped by our background and belief systems, our upbringing, role models and attitudes towards spending, saving and investing. In some cases, these attitudes and beliefs limit our financial outcomes without our even realising it.

In my experience as a financial adviser, I have come to believe that whether or not we will achieve financial freedom is 95 per cent determined by our behaviours, with only 5 per cent attributable to the technical strategies that someone like me can help put in place.

Sounds crazy? Sounds like a financial adviser is not that important? Not at all. If you can get the 95 per cent right, then that 5 per cent will make a huge difference. But at the end of the day, if we can't change our behaviours, attitudes and beliefs, it doesn't matter how perfect our plan, nothing will come of it.

What makes us tick?

Over the years, many financial advisers have come to recognise just how much an individual's upbringing impacts on their current financial situation—good or bad. In our practice we now spend a huge amount of time getting to know what makes our clients tick, identifying patterns of behaviour in relation to money that are positive and negative, and working a sort of financial coaching into the planning process. Much of our time with clients during face-to-face meetings focuses on what has been called 'the psychology of money', while only about 5 per cent is dedicated to the strategic and technical side. Of course, a lot more technical and strategic planning goes on behind the scenes, but I've learned that ultimately if we don't work on the fluffy stuff when we're with our clients, the numbers just won't stack up anyway.

Case study: Jessica's story

Early on in my career, I worked with a young professional woman who for many years just couldn't stick to the credit card repayment plan we had in place for her. I watched on as, year on year, her debt just kept growing (not a lot, but little by little). Every time we sat down and went through the numbers she'd get motivated again for a month or two, before going back to her usual spending patterns.

I started to really question myself as a financial adviser, as I felt completely useless to Jessica and just didn't seem to be adding any value. After going over and over it in my mind, I decided that the next time we sat down I would have a really good talk with her about her level of debt and why we weren't getting anywhere. I was reaching out to her, looking for a way that I could help; otherwise, I felt, it might have been time to end the relationship.

What it came down to, I learned after we'd had our long talk, was that she actually didn't worry at all about her debt! The only time she ever thought about it was when she was in my office; the rest of the time she just completely switched off to it.

This was completely different from what I'd expected, as I'd remembered back to my early adult years when I had found my credit card debt so stressful I couldn't sleep at night. It was a great reminder for me that we can't assume that everyone approaches things in the same way we do.

Together we worked through the situation. In a nutshell, Jessica knew that the debt was not a good thing and understood the numbers when I put them in front of her, but because her day-to-day life wasn't affected by it, once our appointment was over she would quickly put it out of her mind. We started talking about what she hoped to achieve in the future: she had dreams of one day launching her own business and had some brilliant ideas. But she'd never had a dollar to her name, so she accepted that her well-thought-out plan was no more than a pipe dream.

Bingo! I had found the key that could potentially help change her behaviour. This big goal of hers that she felt so passionate about could potentially be just the thing to get her over the line. In the past her ambition had been restricted to 'paying off my credit cards'. Not very exciting, huh? We talked about the fact that she could one day realise her dream if only she could stick to the credit card repayment plan. As we talked, it dawned on me that Jessica had probably never in her life saved for anything and seen money build up (in the right direction at least) in a bank account or investment. I was right, she hadn't.

The common wisdom is that you should always aim to repay expensive debt *before* starting a savings or investment plan, but that strategy just wasn't working. So together we changed our approach. We kept the credit card repayment plan in place, but we started a small share portfolio that she began chipping into—just a few hundred dollars each month—despite the fact that the numbers didn't really make sense.

It turned out to have been the best decision we could have made. Jessica's credit card spending didn't really let up for quite some time, but as she started seeing her wealth build up, her confidence grew and she started believing that she really could achieve her goal of owning her own business. Over time, we worked on her spending behaviours and the way she managed her money, and little by little we began to see improvements.

Jessica hasn't launched her business yet, but she now has a positive overall financial position, by just a little, and is much better at controlling her spending. She understands the value of money better, and having experienced the hard slog of turning her negative position around, she's far less likely to let all her work go out the window now for the sake of racking up a bunch of needless expenses on credit.

As a finance professional, I believe it's important to keep learning and adapting. This experience helped me develop the process that Wealth Enhancers is now known for—a process that achieves real results for our clients. Many other professional firms out there are now taking a values-based approach to advice that is very different from the traditional, inflexible technical approach of the past.

It seems crazy to me now that I could ever have provided financial advice any other way, but life is a journey that never ceases to amaze. I know Jessica has completely changed her view of money during the years we have worked together, and I thank her for being part of my journey.

My purpose in telling this story, now we have covered many of the technical areas of financial planning, is to get you thinking about the psychology behind our attitudes towards money, because an understanding of the issues this raises, as discussed in this and the next chapter, will really make a difference to your financial success. Here I want to dig back a little into the common sources of our relationships with money.

Family values

It has always struck me as interesting how often our goals in life are really similar to those of our parents. Perhaps it is because we often strive to create for ourselves the sort of lifestyle we grew up with. This is not necessarily a bad thing, but it is potentially a limiting belief. A limiting belief is a belief we hold so strongly that it essentially prevents us from being able to see the bigger picture or being able to think differently and imagine a different life for ourselves.

Case study: Rick's story

Rick is a client of mine who grew up in a lovely two-storey, three-bedroom home with a pool in a leafy suburb in the east of Melbourne.

He had a happy childhood. His mother worked part time and his father earned a modest salary, but they had worked hard to create a comfortable lifestyle for their family.

Rick was lucky enough to get into a good university and became an engineer. He was intelligent and possessed a strong work ethic, so he soon rose through the ranks at his firm. He was now heading up a new department and earning a very good income. Interestingly, though, financially he had not thought beyond buying a house (similar to the one he grew up in) and establishing for himself and his family a lifestyle that was almost identical to the one he had enjoyed as a child.

The point of this is not that his parents' lifestyle was not worth emulating, but that Rick hadn't actually ever stopped to think about what he (and his wife and children) really wanted out of life. What were their individual goals, and were they doing everything in their power to create their desired lifestyle for themselves?

We discussed the idea of their spending a month overseas each year as a family. He had travelled a little during university and knew this experience would be positive for the children's development, and given that he worked so hard most of the year it would be a welcome break for him too. But before we discussed it, he'd never even considered such an option was possible. He had never been on an overseas trip with his family when he was growing up, and holidays were generally few and far between.

Fortunately for Rick, they were now in a position to start doing this each year, and the fact that they hadn't overextended themselves with their mortgage and living expenses paid off in the long term. For this family, the important decisions weren't about the house, the pool or the cars, so much as the schools they chose for their children and the way they chose to spend their family time.

Approaches to money

Our upbringing and the belief system we inherit can play out most obviously in the way we feel about money and our attitude towards spending and saving it. It is often in high school or university that we first start managing our own money to some degree — money we perhaps received through an allowance from our parents or part-time jobs or even a Centrelink payment related to study. Chances are, each of us managed our money slightly differently, and this usually owed much to how we grew up, our parents' attitude to money and what they taught us.

Remembering back to my high-school days, and my three closest girlfriends, we each approached money in a completely different way. I was a bit of a spendthrift day by day and often didn't think about whether or not I was receiving fair value for my money, but I was good at setting aside money towards a specific savings target. Two of the other girls saved practically every penny they earned, but they were still different in their approach to spending. One spent very little, and only on bare necessities; the other would splurge on certain things she really wanted but was never wasteful the way I could be sometimes. For my other friend, money ran through her fingers like water and she was never good at saving — and never seemed to have any money to spend either.

For the most part, these attitudes towards money could be traced back home in one way or another. In my case, my parents had done a great job of teaching me to save money, but they never really saved money themselves and generally lived week to week. I also experienced two extremes in my childhood: a fairly comfortable upbringing while my parents were still married, then a big change when they divorced.

After their separation my mum couldn't find a job for almost a year. She had always worked in the family business and didn't have a high level of tertiary education. Although very intelligent, with an exceptional work ethic, as a 48-year-old single mum with two daughters in primary school she wasn't a hot prospect for potential employers. Eventually she found part-time work, which ultimately turned into a successful full-time career, but for the rest of my teenage years things were fairly tight financially and my sister and I each worked from the age of 14.

All my friends had different experiences growing up that helped explain their attitude to money. For all of us, as for any young adult, we needed to learn better ways to manage money. Unfortunately, in our society discussing money matters, even with friends or family, is generally considered inappropriate or embarrassing. So we tend to fight our financial battles alone, and our development is often limited by the fact that we have no-one to bounce ideas off, share our victories with, or simply understand and support us.

Exercise: My money traits

Think about your attitude to money, and how your upbringing has contributed to your current financial situation. Using table 12.1, write down what you believe to be your good behaviours in relation to money and where you think they came from, then do the same for the bad behaviours. In the next column, brainstorm some ideas for what you could do to change those bad behaviours.

Table 12.1: changing our financial traits

My positive financial traits		
Trait	**Why?**	**How can I maximise these?**
My negative financial traits		
Trait	**Why?**	**How can I minimise these?**

Use this exercise as an opportunity to reflect on the sources of your current attitudes towards money. Often simply gaining a deeper understanding of why we act in a certain way is enough to kick the wheels of change into motion.

Learning from experience—some advice for parents

I'm not a parent, so I'm certainly not going to start telling people how to bring up their children! Based on my own experiences with money and as a financial adviser, however, I am comfortable sharing some tips that I believe could have a positive impact on your children's future financial prospects.

Financial literacy programs are still fairly rare in Australian schools. It is important for parents to recognise that most of what our children learn about money will be learned at home. I can say this with confidence because in almost every new client meeting I have, we end up talking about how their parents approached money and what impact that has had on them. More often than not it is a major shaping factor.

Ideally, lead by example

If we are ourselves good financial managers and have managed to build wealth, save for a rainy day, avoid bad debt and generally not be wasteful with money, then one of the most important things we can do is have these conversations with our children. Explain to them how we make daily financial decisions. Explain that money is not unlimited and that a major part of life is balancing what comes in with what goes out and what is set aside. Talk about setting goals and saving, being prudent and demanding value in return for everything we spend money on.

Failing that, do as I say, not as I do!

If we are not that great with our money and tend towards ingrained bad habits, as discussed in the next chapter (and this book will certainly help us change that), this is no excuse for not educating our children. They can still develop good habits, even if we don't always manage to stick to them ourselves. Of course leading by example is better, but even if we ourselves have yet to master the art of saving, talking about being sensible with money and helping our children establish good saving habits is valuable. Discuss with them the importance of putting money aside for a rainy day, not being wasteful and not spending everything they earn.

Some age-specific approaches

Different approaches may prove more beneficial at different ages. Below are some ideas we can use to help our children develop a sensible approach to money that is relevant to their age.

Younger children

Pocket money (a small amount received weekly or monthly) is a great way for children to start learning the basics of money management. These begin with making decisions around how the money will be spent, but encourage them to save a portion of it. Discuss the benefits of putting half into a bank account each week to save for something they particularly want. For example, they might spend $5 a week while banking $5.

Suggest they write down the item they are saving for, along with the amount they need to save, then put this up on their bedroom wall. It will be a great motivational reminder for them. You could make an activity out of it, getting them to create a mini vision board with magazine cutouts and colouring-in pencils, or even create one on a computer or electronic tablet.

Early teens

As the children get older, and their outings with friends start to cost more, providing them with a weekly allowance in return for performing an agreed list of chores will give them a bit of independence. It will also help them to develop an understanding that 'money doesn't grow on trees' and that we need to work to fund our lifestyle. Encourage them to keep saving each week as they have in the past. Suggest they save a little more to accumulate enough for a bigger goal. Again, creating a vision board to represent what they are saving for can be extremely motivating.

Late teens

From roughly age 15, your teens are able to start working in a casual job. Entering the workforce early (even for, say, a single four-hour shift a week) provides precious skills not otherwise learned until later in life, something future employers will value greatly. At this stage I suggest stopping, or reducing, their allowance but encouraging them to continue to save money for things they really want and to spend only what's left on social activities. It might feel tough sending your children off to work and cutting off their allowance, but providing them with the opportunity to develop a good work ethic and money management skills is a far greater gift for the long term than spoiling them now.

To develop their decision-making skills further, introduce them to the 50/25/25 rule. The idea is that now they are earning a basic wage they save 50 per cent of what they earn, spend 25 per cent on sensible items that fall into the 'need' category and have fun with the other 25 per cent. They can still splurge on fun things, but at the same time they learn to demand value. This is simply smart and means they avoid being ripped off, but it also means they start to take responsibility for some of their 'needs' items instead of you covering them all.

Encourage them to come up with a couple of savings goals, one short term and another much longer term goal. Depending on how you feel about social media, Pinterest (www.pinterest.com) can be a great tool for creating an online vision board or goals board. Using this, or even just magazine cutouts again, to create an image of what they are setting money aside for will keep them on track and discourage them from dipping into their savings unnecessarily.

Young adults

As children move past high school or university and enter the workforce full time, many parents will want to see them establish themselves financially and will want to play a role in this.

First Home Saver Accounts (FHSA) are a great government initiative that can form part of the savings process. The government will pay an additional 17 per cent income for four years on any contributions into an FHSA, up to the value of $6000. Any Australian aged 18 and older can establish an FHSA with any current bank, or another bank that offers the product, and set up a regular automatic transfer directly into the account.

The earlier they start, the better, as the FHSA is a four-year investment. The money must stay in the FHSA until the four-year period is up and can then be used as a home deposit. It's important to note that the money can't be used for anything else, and if a home isn't purchased the money can only go into the owner's superannuation fund, which is not necessarily a bad thing, but may not be appropriate in all situations.

I also favour the dollar-for-dollar matching approach to helping kids reach their savings targets, as this certainly adds to their incentive to save. In the case of an FHSA, they could put in $2750 and you could match it. This works out to around $52 a week, which even some university students could afford. Alternatively, you could use the dollar-for-dollar approach in a normal high-interest savings account to help them save for any other goal, such as their first car or an overseas holiday.

Key points

→ Our upbringing shapes our attitude towards money, but we can change this.

→ Identifying your traits, beliefs and attitudes can help you overcome those that may be limiting you.

→ Hang on to what's working, and work on what you could be doing better.

→ Pass on good money management skills to your children.

Putting it into action

Identify your limiting beliefs

It's fairly likely that we all have at least one, if not several, limiting beliefs that we've adopted from our upbringing. To achieve more, we'll need to shake these beliefs and start thinking more broadly. The first step in overcoming our limiting beliefs is simply to identify them, because until now we probably haven't even realised we have them.

Write down any regular thoughts you have that start with 'I can't', 'I won't', 'I'll never', 'It's hard'—or anything along those lines. Ask yourself if you truly believe what you are telling yourself. Are you absolutely certain that *you'll never, you can't, you won't* or *it's too hard*? The chances are that just by challenging yourself in this way, you may start to think a little differently.

In order to overcome your limiting beliefs you'll now need to turn those negative thoughts around and repeat them over and over, in a new positive frame: *I will, I can, it's easy* or at least *it's possible*. Start to imagine overcoming whatever it was that has been holding you back.

CHAPTER 13

Bad
habits

Successful people are simply those with successful habits.

Brian Tracy

They say it takes 30 days to form or to break a habit—that for 30 days you need to focus on something with the determination to change it, until the new behaviour feels natural to you. Essentially, your attitudes, approaches and behaviours with money (based on past traits) are all just habits—habits that can be broken, changed or developed in positive ways.

When I was in high school one of the part-time jobs I had was working in a petrol station in Woolloongabba, Brisbane. I'd wake up at 5 am to get ready to start work at 6 am for an eight-hour shift that finished at 2 pm. I didn't mind the job because it paid much better than Red Rooster (where all my friends worked) and meant I could save up faster to buy my first car. I ended up buying it before I'd even sat my driving test. I got my licence a couple of weeks later and I was off. Like any teenager, I loved the freedom my car gave me and I drove everywhere.

My bad habits

I'd fill up the tank at the end of my shift and grab a cold drink from the service station fridge and whatever chocolate bar I'd been eyeing off.

It started right there and became a habit that stuck with me for the next 10 years: fill up the car, buy a cold drink and a snack—every single time. For years and years I was adding that small cost to my weekly fuel bill. Not a big deal? You might even do something like this yourself, but a couple of years ago I stopped to work out just what a big deal it had become. I was on a long drive to see a client out in the country while working in the family business. My dad was driving and we pulled into a petrol station to refuel. Habit kicked in, and while Dad was filling up the car I grabbed the $2.50 in change that was sitting on the console of the car and ran inside to grab a cold drink. Here I was at a fuel station—I couldn't just sit around in the car waiting, right? Must have a cold drink!

But $2.50 wouldn't buy me any drink, not even a bottle of water (that's right, the stuff that's more or less free out of the tap). Cold drinks were at least $4, with some pushing the $5 mark. Snacks were about the same. Shocked, and feeling a little silly, I skulked back to the car and then started doing the numbers.

I'd filled up my car roughly once a week, or 52 times a year, for approximately 10 years, and every time I'd been adding about $10 to the fuel bill. That's right, I'd spent an additional $5200 as part of my weekly fuel bill for no real return. If I was completely honest with myself, I got no real joy out of these purchases at the overpriced but conveniently located petrol station shop. Half the time I wasn't even thirsty. It was simply habit.

The moral of the story isn't to never buy anything from a petrol station or convenience store, but rather to ask yourself, especially with habitual purchases, am I receiving value for money? Is that something I need, or at least *really* want, and am I happy to pay that price for it right now?

I do still occasionally buy a refreshing cold drink at a petrol station, but usually only when I'm on a long road trip or I'm genuinely thirsty and on the run. The other thing I started to do from that moment on is to *check the bill* . . . which brings me to my other bad habit!

It seems obvious, right? But clearly I had not been checking the printout when I filled up the car. With EFTPOS, credit cards and now PayPass, it's so easy not to even acknowledge the total of your bill at the supermarket, convenience store, pharmacy or petrol station, or in all of those other daily circumstances where you purchase multiple items or services in the same transaction. If I had checked the bill once in a while I might have given some thought far earlier to wasting that $10 a week.

Identify your bad money habits

If the very first step in achieving personal financial security is taking responsibility, then it makes sense that we should always check the bill. It isn't something to feel awkward or embarrassed about. Knowing you've actually made an informed decision with every transaction should in fact empower you. Mindlessly paying any bill that's set down in front of you is not a sign of wealth. Far from it, in fact. Our wealthier clients generally demand the most clarity on our fees and what they will receive in return. They ask questions until they are comfortable they have all the information they need to make a decision to enter into an agreement with us. It also makes me confident that they take the relationship seriously and that they are committed to creating a positive financial future for themselves.

It's essential to identify bad habits in order to make a conscious decision to change them. Think about any bad habits around money that you might need to work on.

Some common bad money habits

Here I've created a shortlist of common bad habits and offered a few suggestions on how you can break them. You may have some of your own that are worth writing down and brainstorming for possible solutions.

It's my shout . . . always

Are you the person who always shouts everyone at the bar? Although this is generous, you probably don't realise how much it's costing you, and sadly it is more than likely that certain people are taking advantage of your open-handedness and don't repay the favour.

Breaking the habit: Keep your mouth shut when the bill comes around, and simply put your share in the pile instead of grabbing the bill and insisting on paying. It might feel a little unnatural at first, but you will come to realise that people aren't expecting you to pay anyway. If you're at a bar or counter to order, just order for yourself and don't offer to pay for the person standing next to you. Again, this might initially feel uncomfortable, but you'll probably find no-one else even notices. It's okay to shout people from time to time, but be a little more selective so you can be confident that the favour will be returned next time.

I never bother to check the bill

Do you just slide your card across the counter, as I did for so many years? It's not on and has to stop right now!

Breaking the habit: Take responsibility and check the bill every time. It's totally okay to decide not to buy something once it's been rung up, if you don't feel the price is reasonable. This is called not being a sucker and will get you ahead far more quickly than completing the transaction resentfully. From now on, don't get out your wallet until you have the bill in your hot little hand. This will stop you from being distracted and simply throwing your card down. While you get your card or cash out of your wallet, quickly scan the bill to check everything is in order. It almost always is, but the added benefit of being more aware of your purchases is that you will become a little more conservative with your spending. The simple act of checking and thinking about each transaction will lead to less mindless spending. You'll feel great for it, and so will your bank balance.

What parking signs?

You find a perfect spot right near the entrance, park the car quickly and head off to your destination, returning a couple of hours later to find a ticket slapped onto your windscreen. Or you're in such a hurry that you slot your car into the one-hour spot, knowing your meeting will run for longer and just hoping you'll be lucky. If this is you, chances are you justify the tickets to yourself with excuses to do with the convenience and time saved being worth the fine! Well, the fine is totally not worth it, I'm telling you right now! It's plain wasted money. You might as well pull a $100 note out of your wallet and toss it in the trash. That's $100 you won't be contributing towards your own financial success.

Breaking the habit: First, check and double check the parking signs. Take a moment each time you park to be sure you're in a legitimate spot and to confirm the time limit and that you've paid the correct fee. Secondly, leave 10 minutes earlier than you normally would to ensure you have time to find an appropriate parking space. You'll be completing your budget in the next chapter, and you'll know exactly how much you should be spending each week, so that parking fine has to come from somewhere. It's going to mean a sacrifice somewhere along the line, because it is an unexpected cost that would otherwise not have occurred.

I'll pay them when I have time

Another bad habit that is so easily avoided is forgetting to pay your bills on time and being slapped with penalty interest or administration charges. I'll admit right now I've even had late fees on parking tickets, which is like a double whammy. Doubly wasteful. If you're struggling to find the funds to pay your bills, then going through the budgeting exercise in the next chapter will help you address this. What I'm really talking about here, though, is simply forgetting to pay on time and paying only once you receive that nasty reminder with the extra fees.

Breaking the habit: I'm all for delaying bill payment to the last possible moment. This will maximise the time you have access to your cash, which is hopefully sitting in a high-interest savings account or a mortgage offset account, meaning you are either earning or saving interest. However, you'll negate that benefit if you then incur a charge on the overdue bill. The best thing to do is log into internet banking as soon as you get the bill, and from your bills account set up the payment to occur just a couple of days before the due date (of course, you need to ensure you have money in the account then). Now it's done, you can forget about the bill until the next one comes around and you have not disadvantaged yourself by paying too soon. Alternatively, and this works well with fixed monthly costs, establish direct debits. Do this only if you're really clear about your costs and you've spent the time working out your budget and setting up your bills account to take care of these costs.

Overdrawn again

One of the disadvantages of having several direct debit agreements in place is that your accounts can end up overdrawn if you don't stay on top of things. Debit accounts can be overdrawn using EFTPOS too, rather than just being declined. Again, these costs need to be covered anyway, and keeping a better check on your bank balances is important to avoid overdrawing the account and incurring completely avoidable fees. Small bank fees like this can rack up to a lot over a year.

Breaking the habit: Establishing your bills account, and ensuring that for each pay cycle you automatically transfer across enough funds to cover your bills is a great starting point. Generally, this is about being more organised. Put a reminder in your diary to check your bank accounts online at least once a week. Creating a list of regular transactions (you will be able to pull this straight from your budget) and placing it somewhere handy will provide you with a good reminder of what's coming up.

Missing out on early bird specials

Early bird specials are the best. So many of us don't want to commit to events in the future, so we'd rather take the chance and book our tickets at the last moment, even though it costs us more.

Breaking the habit: Get organised with your diary and if there's something you really want to go to with an early bird special, just book the ticket now and lock the date away. If you can manage to do this a couple of times a year, you'll often save yourself serious money.

A timely validation

The day after I finished this chapter I had breakfast with Zoe Lamont, the founder of an outstanding financial literacy organisation called 10thousandgirl, and I was oh so glad I checked the bill. There's always the possibility of a mistake, or even fraud, passing unnoticed if you don't check. After we'd finished up, I went to sign the credit card receipt and noted that the person who had rung up the $23.30 bill had also included a $23.30 tip for himself. I chose to assume this was a mistake, but thankfully I picked it up and saved us from paying double the bill.

I'm fairly sure I wouldn't have picked up this error even when I later checked my bank statement as it wasn't a huge amount of money. So I'm relieved that at least on this occasion I practised what I preached and reviewed the bill rather than signing away unquestioningly.

The swapping strategy

One of the best things my partner has taught me is a different way of looking at the value of money. Finn is really good at determining when and what to spend his money on, based on the value he will receive in exchange. His approach is generally focused on the experience. Here's just one simple example from my life.

For many years I had been running at the Tan (a track around the perimeter of Melbourne's Botanical Gardens) with a good friend one morning a week. Following our run, we would go to our favourite cafe for coffee and breakfast. As we got more serious about our running we started meeting twice and then three times a week, and we'd often meet on other days too to do yoga or another type of workout.

I loved being fit and sharing that journey with her, but one of the main reasons I would leap out of bed at 5.30 am was for our catch-up breakfast afterward. It was like a little reward for the effort we were putting in. As you can imagine, though, the $15–$20 each day was really starting to add up now that we had increased our exercise regularity.

We tossed this around and tried to decide if we should keep meeting for our run but only have breakfast once a week. But this took part of the pleasure out of our routine because it removed the element of reward. More importantly, we'd often just have breakfast anyway because we enjoyed the catch-up so much, and obviously this outcome defeated the purpose of trying to save money.

I'm not sure how long it took us to work it out, but one day it dawned on us just to have coffee out and eat breakfast at home. Such a simple solution, and the best part is we have the same experience (30 minutes together in the same cafe as always, chatting and enjoying each other's company) but for about 20 per cent of the cost. We can afford to have four or five coffees each week for the same price as one breakfast and coffee. This is what I refer to as the *swapping strategy:* looking for ways to get the same experience for a reduced—or even better, no—cost.

Finn is excellent at this. He never wastes money on frivolous items that provide no real value or return, things that simply don't contribute to his life. He would never buy bottled water, for example. It's really no different from that out of the tap, the plastic bottles are terrible for the environment, and it's pretty easy to carry around a drink bottle in your bag or car. Buying bottled water adds no value to your life.

He never pays full price for homewares—things like linen, towels, kitchen utensils, even furniture. You really don't need the latest can opener, which is exactly the same as last year's model but black instead of white. These things aren't fashion accessories to replace each season, so there's really no point in paying extra for the latest model. The same goes for basic clothes: he never pays full price for underwear or running shoes or exercise gear. It has no significant impact on your life whether you have Asics GEL-Kayano 17s or 18s.

So what should you spend money on? What does change your life? Technology for one. I don't mean you need to camp out to get the latest smart phone, and you can surely live without it for a month or two, but the reality is that advances in this kind of technology can often facilitate improvements to your life. That's worth spending money on.

Here are some easy swapping ideas:

- Drink tap water with your meal at a restaurant, instead of ordering bottled water or an expensive soft drink or juice. Same experience, lower cost.

- Take leftovers to work, instead of buying lunch. Take it to the park, instead of the usual cafe—a different but possibly even nicer experience.

- Cancel your gym membership and work out or run outdoors—so much nicer, and easier on the hip pocket.

- Walk or take public transport to work instead of driving and paying for parking.

- Borrow books from the library, or swap with friends, instead of always buying new ones.

- If you're addicted to magazines, cut a deal with your friends to buy a different publication each and swap them during the month.

- Stream internet from your phone, instead of having a separate connection for all your devices. Of course, be sure to check your current plan, and ensure it's not too expensive to do this, although unlimited plans are now common.

- Catch up with friends over coffee instead of breakfast or lunch.

Exercise: Value-for-money diary

Test yourself for a week. Every time you decide to spend money on anything at all, consider the value it is adding to your life in return for the cost. If the answer is little to none, then ditch the purchase.

An easy way to approach this is to keep a value-for-money diary and make a note of what the cost was and what you got in return. The simple act of recording the transactions will help you reflect on whether or not you really got value for your money.

My secret weapon

Quality over quantity has always been my little personal secret weapon. When I was much younger I remember hitting a huge clothing warehouse sale. I shopped till I dropped and came home with innumerable absolute bargains. And I never wore any of them. Why? Easy. I'd bought them because they were going cheap, not because I really wanted them. I've never bought on sale 'just because' since.

Sales are a fantastic bonus when you already had that item on your list, and certainly worth seeking out for homewares or underwear or other items you may need regularly. But when it comes to sale shopping, remember to ask yourself, 'Do I love this, and would I pay full price for it?' If you can honestly answer yes, then go ahead. Otherwise, leave it behind.

While studying and working in a bar part time, I fell in love with a beautiful woollen jumper from Alannah Hill. I was still young and Alannah Hill didn't exactly fit into my budget, but I saved and saved and eventually bought that jumper. I loved it for six years and wore it until it was on its last legs. Now that's what I call value, and a bargain too, in terms of cost per wear. Far better than the hideous $10 lime green singlet I bought in the warehouse sale and could barely bring myself to wear.

When you buy quality items, you often find you crave less. You will look after, and derive more pleasure from, a small number of beautiful items of clothing, than any amount of poorly made cheap junk.

With a firmer grip on your spending behaviours, it's time now to take stock—to develop a detailed picture of your current financial position, which is the subject of the following chapter—before putting your financial plan in place (chapter 15).

Key points

→ We all have habits, but bad ones can always be broken and good ones can always be formed.

→ Taking responsibility includes checking the bill.

→ Demand value for money with everything you purchase.

→ Look for ways to get the same experience for a lower cost.

Putting it into action

We all have bad habits and attempting to change them all at once is a tough ask. An effective way to form a series of new habits is to focus on one habit at a time. This approach is in line with slow money thinking, and is a far more sustainable way to creating lasting improvements.

Write down the top three bad habits you would like to change, pick the one you'd like to tackle first and write the current month next to it, then write the next month next to the second habit you'd like to change, and so on. For the next 30 days all you need to do is work on changing that first habit you've chosen. Spend some time now considering how you will change your bad habit into a good habit and visualise the different moments coming up where you will have the opportunity to exercise your new behaviours. This will prepare you and ensure you are ready to change when the time comes.

CHAPTER 14

Take
stock

What is not started today is never finished tomorrow.

Johann Wolfgang von Goethe

Before we set out to achieve anything in life, it's important to know where we currently are. In many ways, achieving financial success can be compared with attaining a health or fitness goal, For example, if we wanted to run a marathon, we would first need to assess our current fitness level, then build a plan for how we would ultimately reach our goal of running 42.2 kilometres. If we are currently running 5 km comfortably, we will likely have more work to do than if we have recently completed a half-marathon distance of 21.1 km. Either way, we will need to come up with a training program that will see our fitness increase week by week, until we can make that final distance and reach our marathon goal.

Building wealth is the same. First we must determine what we currently own, identify what we owe, look at what we earn and have a clear picture of what we are spending, before drawing up a plan to reach our goal. In the next chapter we'll discuss goal setting, but for now we'll focus on developing a clear picture of our current financial position.

Where are we now?

To determine our current financial position, we must establish:

- how much we earn
- how much we spend
- what's left over
- what we own
- what we owe.

The relationship between these five factors is really important. How much we earn less how much we spend should (actually must) give us a positive figure representing the leftover amount. This surplus is what we use to get us from what we currently own and owe to where we want to be, which means reaching our goal!

Without facing all these factors and developing a clear understanding of our current financial situation, we will struggle to make the necessary positive changes. Remember, it's always challenging to make big changes in life, but great rewards will follow. Nothing comes easy, but hard work, discipline and focus will pay off in the end.

The golden rule

The golden rule that every one of us needs to internalise to create financial security is really simple. It's so simple that it seems almost ridiculous to have to say it, although based on the financial position of many in the world today, it is a principle that generally seems to have been forgotten.

Spend less than you earn!

There, I've said it. We live in a world where credit is easy to come by and consumerism is king. Over the past few years, ABS figures show a decrease in consumer spending and an increase in the household savings rate for the first time in many years. This means that as a nation we are starting to get the message, which is great news. Figure 14.1 tracks the household savings ratio (savings per disposable income), indicating that from 1980 it fell fairly steadily, reducing to a point below 0 per cent in the early noughties. We can also see a sharp increase following the GFC in 2008.

Figure 14.1: household savings ration, 1980–2010

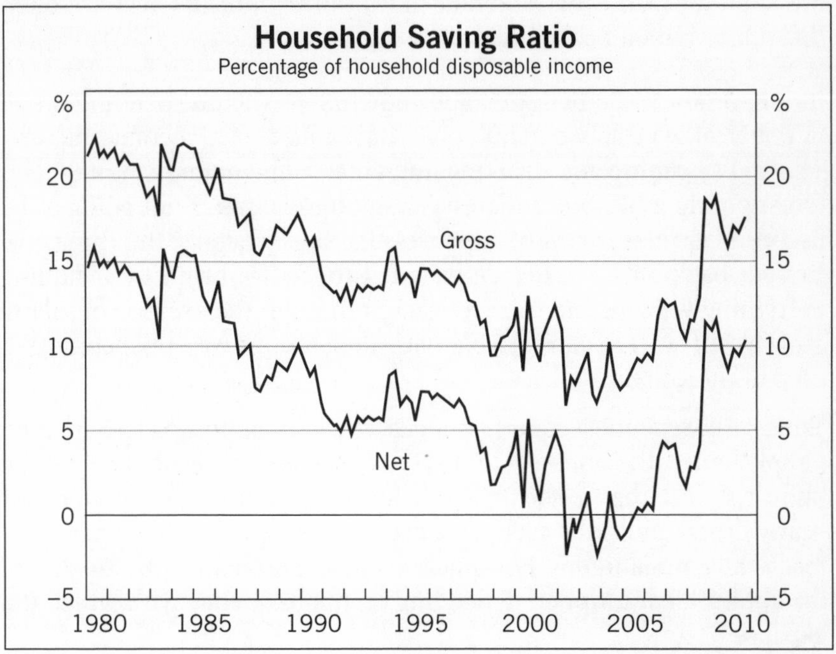

Source: ABS data used with permission from the Australian Bureau of Statistics www.abs.gov.au.

From my experience, one of the main reasons we overspend is that we simply don't keep track of where our money is going. When we have a few credit cards and a couple of debit cards, and are paying for everything online or using EFTPOS, it's easy just to spend away without thinking about it. We often don't stop to consider what things truly cost, accepting on face value the prices listed. So the first step, and it's not an easy one to take, is to complete a budget and face up to how much we are spending on everything in our life.

Completing a budget

Essentially, a budget is a snapshot of our total income that calculates all of our expenses. It really isn't as painful to prepare as it sounds and can usually be completed in about 15 minutes! That said, it's important that our estimate is as accurate as possible, so it's best to get together any bills or irregular expenses that occur to ensure we have a good starting point. Electricity and gas bills, car registration, insurances and the like that turn up at different times throughout the year are often difficult to remember off the top of our heads.

It's important to be realistic about how much we are spending on all of the weekly costs we incur so we can build up an accurate picture. Things like dining and drinking out, entertainment and clothing tend to vary quite a bit, but underestimating these costs is not going to be useful. It is these types of expenses that are generally the things we can cut back on if we decide we need to. So we begin by including everything we can, and then we can go through the exercise of asking ourselves if we are comfortable with the amount we are spending in each of these areas.

Table 14.2 sets out a sample budget that we can complete on paper. Simply enter the income or expense relevant to each line of the budget, select the period (weekly, fortnightly, monthly, quarterly or yearly) then multiply each expense by the appropriate amount to reach the annual figure. For quick reference, use table 14.1 to choose the applicable multiplier, depending on the frequency with which the expense occurs.

Table 14.1: frequency multipliers

Frequency	Multiply by
Weekly (W)	52
Fortnightly (F)	26
Monthly (M)	12
Quarterly (Q)	4
Yearly (Y)	1

If, say, we shop for groceries every two weeks and spend about $320, our annual grocery bill will be $320 × 26 = $8320.

Table 14.2: a sample budget

Income	Amount $	Frequency	Annual $
Net income (after tax)	_____	W / F / M / Q / Y	_____
Other income (after tax)	_____	W / F / M / Q / Y	_____
		Total income	**$_____**

Expenses	Amount $	Frequency	Annual $
Dining out	_____	W / F / M / Q / Y	_____
Drinking out	_____	W / F / M / Q / Y	_____
Coffee/tea out	_____	W / F / M / Q / Y	_____
Groceries	_____	W / F / M / Q / Y	_____
Clothing	_____	W / F / M / Q / Y	_____
Public transport	_____	W / F / M / Q / Y	_____
Fuel	_____	W / F / M / Q / Y	_____
Car insurance and registration	_____	W / F / M / Q / Y	_____
Car loan repayments	_____	W / F / M / Q / Y	_____
Rent/mortgage repayments	_____	W / F / M / Q / Y	_____
House and contents insurance	_____	W / F / M / Q / Y	_____
Electricity	_____	W / F / M / Q / Y	_____
Phone	_____	W / F / M / Q / Y	_____
Gas	_____	W / F / M / Q / Y	_____
Internet	_____	W / F / M / Q / Y	_____
Gym membership	_____	W / F / M / Q / Y	_____
Clubs/subscriptions	_____	W / F / M / Q / Y	_____
Health insurance	_____	W / F / M / Q / Y	_____
Personal insurances	_____	W / F / M / Q / Y	_____
Personal loan repayments	_____	W / F / M / Q / Y	_____

(continued)

Table 14.2: a sample budget (*cont'd*)

Expenses	Amount $	Frequency	Annual $
Other:_____	_____	W / F / M / Q / Y	_____
Other: _____	_____	W / F / M / Q / Y	_____
Other: _____	_____	W / F / M / Q / Y	_____
		Total expenses	**$_____**
		Total income	**$_____**
		Less: total expenses	**$_____**
		Equals: surplus	**$_____**

Looking for something more tech-savvy?

If you sign up for my newsletter at www.sarahriegelhuth.com.au I will send you a budgeting tool you can use to complete this process. The tool is in Excel format and is really simple to use, and it does all the adding up for you so you won't need a calculator. I'll also send you a financial position tool you can use in the next step.

The tool includes a huge list of possible items, as well as a section where you can add items that do not appear on the list. Enter each of your expenses then use the drop-down list to select its regularity and it will total up the expenses for you. Your total income, expenses and any resulting surplus will be displayed at the bottom of the page.

Once you have completed your budget, you will have a better idea of where your money goes and what is left over. Remember, the surplus is what you can use to improve your financial position, increase your overall wealth and progress towards your goal.

Choices and compromises

Now you have completed your budget, you may be looking at some of the figures in shock! Often we don't realise just how much we are spending on certain things. This is the time to sit down and have a good hard chat with yourself! For any items that stand out to you, ask yourself, are you receiving real value for that expense? Do you feel it is a reasonable amount of money to be spending, and is it something that you simply couldn't give up? If the answer is yes, then fine. But if the answer is no, or even maybe, then it's time to make the decision, from today forward, what you actually want to allow yourself to spend on that expense item.

Let's say we eat out each day for lunch, five days a week at a cost of about $15 a day, so $75 each week. If we multiply the $75 by about 48 working weeks in a year, our total lunch costs are $3600. Potentially, if in fact those lunches aren't critical to our happiness (they could be), this is an area where we could cut back. Assuming we have been doing this mostly out of habit, yet we perhaps haven't taken a decent holiday in years as we never seemed to have the money for it, if we cut back to two lunches each week we've located more than $2000 that could be put towards a great getaway within the next 12 months.

What else could we cut back on? It's unlikely we'll want to cut out many items completely, but if we rework our budget after finding a couple of expenses we can cut back on, we'll be surprised to find how much bigger our surplus becomes.

Completing a financial position assessment

Now we have completed our budget, we are ready to face the next challenge, and depending on what we have been doing with our money in the past, this will be either an exciting or a daunting experience. Remember the exercise we did earlier where we added up our average earnings? Well, now is the moment of truth. What have we been doing with our hard-earned cash?

Our financial position is simply the total value of our personal wealth. It can be positive or negative, or even zero. It is what it is, and the only way to make it bigger (to reach our goal) is to face up to where we are now. So let's get started.

Assets and liabilities

The first thing we need to write down is all our assets—that is, what we own. An asset is really only an asset if it has a resale value, and if it is something we would sell in order to reach our goals. For this reason we generally don't consider a vehicle to be an asset, because we most often need it to get around. We probably wouldn't sell it other than to replace it, and it costs us money while going down in value over time.

What we're looking for here is tangible things that form part of our wealth and will help us reach our goal—things like money in the bank, shares or managed funds, superannuation balances, property and, at a stretch, collectable items such as paintings or stamps that have a realistic market value that could (and would) be realised when required. All of these items need to be added to the left-hand side of table 14.3 before being totalled up at the bottom.

The next thing we need to determine is our liabilities—that is, our loans and credit cards, any money at all that we owe, including to a friend or family member, and any large bills that we have yet to pay. Include everything. Everything! We total up all of the items listed in the liabilities column.

At the bottom of the table we subtract our total liabilities from our total assets. This will give us our financial position, which will reflect our total net wealth, what we are worth and essentially what we have done with all of our income over the years.

Table 14.3: calculating our financial position

Assets	Value $	Liabilities	Value $
Cash	_____	Credit cards	_____
Shares	_____	Personal loan	_____
Managed funds	_____	Car loan	_____
Property	_____	Mortgage	_____
Superannuation	_____	Other:	_____
Other:	_____	Other:	_____
Other:	_____	Other:	_____
Total assets	**$_____**	**Total liabilities**	**$_____**
Financial position (total assets – total liabilities)			**$_____**

Outcomes

If you've signed up for my newsletter (www.sarahriegelhuth.com.au), you will have received an Excel tool that looks similar to table 14.3, and you can use this to automatically calculate your overall financial position. The resulting total will reflect one of the following three possible outcomes.

- *Outcome 1: a positive financial position.* If you've added up everything you own, then subtracted any money you owe, and you've arrived at a positive figure, then you can pat yourself on the back. This is great news and means you are ahead of many. The next chapter on goal setting is going to help you work out where you need to get to from here, and what the difference is between your goal and your current position.

- *Outcome 2: a neutral financial position.* If you are bang on zero then look at it as a clean slate, and the only way to go is up. You are in a great position to start building your wealth and pursuing your goals. The most important thing is to start thinking big and to continue to maintain control of your finances so your financial position improves over time.

- *Outcome 3: a negative financial position.* If you are in this boat, don't despair. Now is the time to recognise your situation and to start turning it around and creeping towards a positive financial position. Remember not to set your sights on zero but to start thinking about actually building wealth that will allow you ultimately to reach your goal. You'll need to get to zero first, but it's only one point on the greater journey to a positive financial position.

No matter what financial position we are in, it's still important to review our liabilities and to ensure we don't have any of the bad debt discussed in chapter 4. Bad debt is debt that results from lifestyle expenses we can't afford or is attached to an asset that is only going down in value (such as credit cards, car loans and personal loans). Bad debt is just costing us money in the form of high interest rates and is blocking our path to achieving our goals and dreams.

If we have any of these bad debts, debts that aren't working for us, we will need to focus on smashing them down using our leftover income when we set our goals in the next chapter. Remember, with a little focus and discipline everything is possible, and we'll be hitting our personal targets in no time at all.

Effective cash management

There is no perfect way to structure your bank accounts and flow of money. Different people set up their bank accounts, spending and savings structures in different ways. However, the following will provide you with a clear and simple starting point that works.

Once you have completed your budget you will be able to identify three important figures: your regular weekly expenses, your irregular expenses such as bills, and the surplus (which is what you can allocate to debt repayment, savings and investments). Let's call the first two items 'personal spending' and 'bills'.

Your personal spending comprises any expense that occurs weekly and includes things like dining out, socialising and food, but also petrol and parking—basically anything for which you need ready access to funds on a regular basis.

Your bills consist mainly of items that occur irregularly or at monthly or quarterly intervals, such as rent, electricity, phone bills and insurance. Generally these are things for which a direct debit can be established, or a bill is sent and needn't be paid the moment the expense is incurred.

Establish the following segregated accounts:

- *Bills account.* Establish an account that can receive your salary and from which all your direct debits can be drawn. This account acts as a kind of hub into and out of which all your money will flow.

- *Personal spending account.* Establish a second account that receives a transfer from your bills account each week to cover all of the weekly expenses that you identified in your budget. You can also use a credit card for this if you are very disciplined and able to stick to spending only the amount you have budgeted.

- *Online savings account (with sub-accounts).* For your short-term savings goals establish a high-interest online savings account, preferably with a separate institution and with a sub-account facility for separating your savings goals. Set up an automatic monthly transfer from your bills account into each sub-account related to a separate savings goal (you'll learn more about this in the next chapter).

- *Investments and superannuation.* Your surplus will be further used to contribute to any investments or to your superannuation. These transfers should also come from your bills account on a regular basis.

This structure should make it really easy for you to stick to your plan, repay debt and build wealth. Provided you have been accurate when completing your budget, there will always be enough money in your bills account to fund all of your expenses, savings and expenses. Better yet, because you have set everything up to take care of itself automatically, all you need to worry about is sticking to the amount allocated weekly to your personal spending account.

It's best to leave a little room to move, so overestimating your bills and irregular expenses just a little is a good idea in the beginning. You may need to check your bills account from time to time, just to be sure nothing has gone wrong with your direct debits or automatic transfers, and if you find you have accumulated more than expected, you can always allocate the extra to one of your savings goals.

Knowing where you stand financially is a critical first step in any good financial plan. Establishing sound cash management structures will help you keep a better eye on where your money is going and will play a big part in helping you stay within your budget.

Perhaps no issue is of more fundamental importance in financial planning than personal goal setting, which is the subject of the next chapter.

Key points

→ You need to face where you are now in order to build a reliable plan for the future.

→ Budgeting isn't really scary and takes less time than you think!

→ What you earn less what you spend should give you a surplus.

→ What you own less what you owe is your financial position, or net worth. This figure should be positive.

Putting it into action

Complete the budget and financial position assessment using either the tables in this chapter or the Excel tools on my website, and take the time to restructure your bank accounts. (Start with your 'personal spending' and 'bills' accounts and in the next chapter, once you have set your goals, you will be able to establish appropriate allocations to your high-interest online savings accounts.)

It's a good idea to do this regularly—say, every three months—as this will keep you motivated as you track towards your goal. It will also help you make decisions about increasing your spending in any areas, as you will start to get a feel for the impact this will have on your overall financial situation.

CHAPTER 15
Goal
setting

If you don't know where you are going, you'll end up someplace else.

Yogi Berra

Every six months or so I sit down alone and conduct a big personal brainstorming session on what I want to achieve in the months ahead (and beyond). I'm sure we have all heard the claim that writing our goals down gives us a 95 per cent chance of achieving them. Amazingly, I have found this to be true throughout my life. I have also found that if we then display these written goals in a place where we will look at them every day, we increase our chances of success even further—to almost 100 per cent.

So why don't we all do this? Well, doing it properly is hard and it's challenging. Setting big goals is never easy, because it demands that we get out there and actually get them done. We're pushing our limits and attempting to achieve something that right now seems scary and difficult, forcing us into the unknown.

One of the great things about writing our goals down is the sense of accomplishment we have when we finally get to tick each one off the list. The simple act of writing it down helps us remember what it felt like when achieving the goal seemed out of reach, and we were scared of it and unsure we could do it. Reviewing our goals once complete rewards us with a feeling of self-belief because we have put our ideas into action.

How, you may wonder, does all this relate to our finances? I believe that in order to achieve true financial freedom, and to remain motivated to improve our financial situation, it's important we set real goals in relation to our money.

Setting goals keep us motivated

The importance of setting specific goals in relation to our money is two-fold. First, it gives us something to work towards, instead of just living payday to payday. Second, if we set our goals correctly we will gain a far deeper understanding of money and come to appreciate that it is simply there to facilitate our life.

I don't believe in setting goals like 'I want $15 000 in the bank' or 'I want a share portfolio worth $500 000' or 'I want four properties worth $2 million'. Why not? Because there is no emotional factor attached to these goals. They are based on mere figures. What we really need to ask ourselves is, 'What lifestyle will owning four properties worth $2 million give me?' That is what the goal should be. Aiming for $15 000 in the bank isn't going to be hugely motivating by itself. If that $15 000 is to pay for a three-month holiday to Europe, however, that's a different story. That could be super-motivating, because every time we even consider dipping into our savings account, or fail to put away our regular savings amount, we would be pushing back our European holiday.

The best financial outcomes I have seen over my career, and from my own personal experience, are reached when we have set a big goal for our life or lifestyle, and then worked out how much we need to save to achieve this.

Start daydreaming

Not sure how to go about this? Grab a pen and paper and start day-dreaming. If money was no object what would you want your life to look like? Create a three-column table similar to table 15.1. Start by writing your goals in the left column, then think about when you want to have achieved each goal, and finally what financial resources you would you need to make it happen. I have included a few suggestions to help you get started.

Table 15.1: establishing our goals

Goal	When?	How much?
Visit Europe for a two-month holiday.	2 years	$12 000
Feel secure that I could survive if I lost my job (repay credit card of $5500 plus three months' salary).	18 months	$21 000
Start a family (would need to set aside at least one year's salary).	5 years	$95 000
Get married.	1 year	$36 000
Complete my master's degree.	4 years	$40 000
Start my own business (with six months' income to cover expenses while the business grows).	2 years	$47 500
Buy a new car.	_____	$_____
Retire at age 50.	_____	$_____
Take a year off to volunteer (would need $500 per week).	_____	$_____

As we can see, all these suggested goals require some level of financial support. This is because money simply facilitates life. Alone it gives us nothing, but having money allows us to follow our dreams and pursue our passions; it enables us to live the life of our choosing instead of feeling trapped by our own financial circumstances.

There's no rule about how many goals we need to set, and it's absolutely fine to have just one. My only rule is that the goal be something tangible that we *really* want for our life, as this is the key ingredient that will help us to stay focused and ultimately reach our goal.

Reaching for our goals

Once we have established the goals we are working towards, we can start to create a plan for achieving them. In chapter 14 we completed a budget that identified the surplus funds we have available each year—that is, the amount left over from our income once all our expenses have been taken out. This is the money we can put to work to help us reach our goals. Table 15.2 sets up an example of someone with three goals. Let's work through it.

Table 15.2: three goals—an example

Goal	When?	How much?
Feel secure that I could survive if I lost my job: • completely repay personal debt of $3000 • have one month's salary of $4200 available for emergency.	1 year	$7200
Visit Europe for a two-month holiday.	2 years	$12000
Start my own consultancy firm.	10 years	$100000

In this case, let's assume a current financial position of −$3000 (no assets and just this small credit card debt) and a surplus each year of $17000 ($1416 in surplus each month). We could approach this challenge in either of two different ways.

Option 1: If we have the discipline to repay our credit card and not use any more credit

Cease using the credit card and focus on repaying the debt over the next two to three months. Each month the surplus of $1416 can be applied directly to the credit card via an automatic BPAY; in three months the card is completely repaid. Now we need to determine how to start on the next goals:

The goal of building an emergency fund of $4200 is now in sight. By dividing this total by the nine months left in the year, we can calculate that we need to save approximately $460 a month to reach our target. As this is a short-term savings goal, a high-interest online savings account would be the best place for this money.

The goal of saving $12000 for a trip to Europe is now 21 months away. If we divide $12000 by 21 months, we will see that $570 a month (plus a little interest) should permit us to reach our goal. This is also a short-term goal that would be most appropriately held in cash.

Choosing a high-interest online savings account that allows us to set up sub-accounts or separate savings buckets is a great way to separate different shorter term savings goals.

Out of the monthly surplus of $1416, there remains $386 to put towards the long-term target of $100 000 to start a consultancy firm. A diversified share portfolio could be a great place to start building this kind of wealth. We will be able to direct $386 a month into the share portfolio in three months' time, once the credit card has been repaid. After the first year, when the goal of establishing an emergency fund has been achieved, a further $460 per month can be directed towards the consultancy fund. I'm sure you get the picture: after two years, when both the previous goals have been achieved, the full $1416 each month can go towards this larger goal, which, based on a rough estimation, should be quite easily attained.

Option 2: If we don't think we have the discipline needed to get our credit card spending under control

Although it won't be the best strategy financially, it might be best to start saving and investing right away in order to build wealth that can ultimately be used to wipe out the credit card debt. We'll need $7200 to do this, so we arrange for $600 ($7200 divided by 12 months) to be automatically transferred each month into a high-interest online savings account (see table 15.3). At the end of 12 months, we will have more than $7200 available with interest earned and will be able to repay the credit card in one lump sum.

Table 15.3: saving to pay off the credit card debt

Surplus	Amount
Monthly surplus	$1416
Less: buffer savings	−$600
Surplus remaining	**$816**

To ensure we're at least covering our minimum credit card repayments and don't incur penalty fees, we will need to set aside perhaps $100 each month (see table 15.4).

Table 15.4: meeting minimum repayments

Surplus	Amount
Monthly surplus	$1416
Less: buffer savings	−$600
Less: credit card min.	−$100
Surplus remaining	**$716**

At the same time, we establish a sub-account attached to this online savings account for the Europe trip, and arrange another automatic transfer of $500 a month into this account (see table 15.5). This regular amount will ensure we have just over $12000 available after two years when interest is included.

Table 15.5: sub-account savings

Surplus	Amount
Monthly surplus	$1416
Less: buffer savings	−$600
Less: credit card min.	−$100
Less: Europe savings	−$500
Surplus remaining	**$216**

Out of the surplus of $1416 each month, there is now $216 that can be put towards the long-term goal of $100000 to start a consultancy firm. Again, as a much longer term goal, a diversified share portfolio would be a great place to start building this kind of wealth.

In this example, we can direct $216 a month into the share portfolio right away (depending on the initial amount required to open it). After the first year, when the emergency fund has been set up and our credit card repaid in full, we will be able to direct a further $700 a month towards building the consultancy firm fund. And, as in option 1, after two years, with the lesser two goals achieved, the full $1416 each month can go towards this larger goal.

Allocating savings to each goal

The examples above give us some ideas of how we can use our surplus to meet our goals. Table 15.6 shows how we can apply this approach to our goals.

Table 15.6: calculating our monthly contributions

Goal	Amount	No. of months	Monthly contribution
1_____	$_____	_____	$_____
2_____	$_____	_____	$_____
3_____	$_____	_____	$_____
	Total monthly contribution		$_____
	Available monthly surplus		$_____
	Difference		$_____

We simply copy in our goal from the previous table, include the amount and then determine the number of months within which we want to reach the goal (multiply the number of years by 12 to come to this figure). To work out the monthly contribution, we simply divide the 'Amount' figure by the figure in the 'No. of months' column.

This calculation doesn't take into account capital growth or income received on our investments, of course. It is simply a starting point to help us work out roughly what we need to set aside. Using online calculators, such as those available on www.infochoice.com.au, can help us narrow down our contribution levels more accurately.

We then need to add up the total in the 'Monthly contributions' column, enter our current 'Available monthly surplus' and subtract the second figure from the first to arrive at the difference. If this figure is positive, it means we can allocate more funds to our most important goal so we will be able to reach it faster. If the number is negative, we will need to think about which goals are more important to us and understand that the time frame on our less important goals may need to be pushed out further. We could also consider areas in which we can cut back on our spending in order to make up the difference.

Prioritising our goals

When establishing multiple goals it is important to prioritise them in order to determine where to direct our focus, especially when we don't have the financial resources to achieve all of them. If this is the case, there's no need to despair — we simply need to focus on our most important goal and work towards that. It's surprising how quickly we'll find things will start to head in the right direction. Remember, a pay rise or increase in income could be just around the corner, and because we now know what our goals are, we'll be sure to put the extra money to good use right away instead of just spending it.

Of course, it is likely that our goals will shift from time to time, which is why it is important to continue to review these goals and make any changes if and when required. We simply follow the same process each time — every three months is a great time frame for these reviews.

The greatest benefit of having a tangible goal, something we really, really want to achieve, is that it stops us from making up excuses to ourselves for why we're spending our money instead of putting it aside for bigger and better things. Do we really want to set back our trip to Europe for the sake of those new clothes? Or put our new business on hold so we can pay for that big night out? Remember, every little bit counts, and this works both ways. Every little bit we put towards our goals will take us one step closer to them, while every little but we spend instead of saving will take us one step further away. It really does all add up.

We now know exactly what we need to do to reach our goals. We can't argue with the numbers, and spending what we should be putting away could easily destroy our well-laid plans. Now we can stop living in fantasyland and telling ourselves we'll start next week, because we've started already and we can no longer turn back. Stick with it! A little short-term pain now will guarantee that some serious long-term gains await us in the future.

The bucket approach

Now you've set your financial goals, it's time to start putting a plan in place to achieve them. The *bucket approach* concept will help you to visualise how your financial resources, over time, can fulfil all of your goals. Here's how it works:

Think of each goal as a bucket. Each bucket will be a different size, depending on the financial resources you will require to reach each goal. Imagine lining up all your buckets, in order of priority, from the most important goal to the least important. Now imagine that all your money is water and each week you are given a jug of water. You need to decide how much of that water should go into each bucket each week in order eventually to fill them all up, but importantly, making sure the highest priority buckets are filled up first.

Taking a simple example, let's say we have five buckets representing five goals:

- pay off credit card ($3000)
- create an emergency fund ($7000)
- save a home deposit ($45 000)
- save for a holiday ($2000)
- save enough for retirement ($1 million).

Now let's think of life as essentially having three main buckets:

- *The emergency bucket.* This bucket means no personal debt and enough cash in the bank to cover approximately three months' salary in case of an emergency.
- *The lifestyle bucket.* This bucket means enough wealth to meet our lifestyle goals before we retire. So throughout our working life all the goals we want to achieve are in this bucket.
- *The retirement bucket.* This bucket means enough wealth to be completely self-sufficient and not reliant on working to earn an income. This is a really important bucket, because if this bucket isn't full by the time we cease working we will be in trouble, as there is no more water coming from anywhere.

At any point in time the first bucket we need to fill is the emergency bucket. This covers our basic needs, so if we don't have this bucket full we are walking on a tightrope, waiting for the wind to blow in the wrong direction. With this bucket empty we will suffer high levels of stress and anxiety. It would essentially mean that our other buckets will never really be filled.

So each week we need to direct most of our water here until we have filled this bucket up. This bucket is pretty boring, as it doesn't really give us anything tangible, other than peace of mind, but focusing on the benefits of being stress free and feeling secure should help us to stay on track. Keeping the bigger picture in mind is important too, because if we can't fill this bucket, we're not going to be able to start on the next one, which is a really fun bucket to fill.

Imagine that you've filled up your emergency bucket to the point where it's starting to overflow. Great news! Now we can direct the water that's overflowing from that bucket into our lifestyle bucket. This is our vision board, where we keep our dreams and the things we hope for in life.

In Australia, 9 per cent of everything we earn automatically goes into our retirement bucket. This means we can relax a little early on and focus on the other two buckets first although, as we discussed in chapter 11, the earlier we can start filling the retirement bucket, the better off we will be in the long term.

Depending on how good we are at managing our money, how big our buckets need to be and the volume of our weekly jug of water, we may decide to tip some water into each bucket. The important thing to remember is that we focus on filling up the emergency bucket first, even if we choose to start filling up the other two at the same time.

I like the visualisation of water flowing into buckets, as it gives me a feeling of abundance when I think about it. A positive state of mind is just as important when we think about money as it is when we think about goal setting and other aspects of our lives. Spend a little time each day imagining your money flowing into those buckets, with each bucket representing the stress-free lifestyle we have chosen for ourselves, the lifestyle that expresses our personal goals and dreams based on what is important to us. A cornerstone of this stress-free lifestyle is good insurance cover, which is the subject of the next chapter.

Key points

→ Set tangible goals based on lifestyle desires, rather than purely on money.

→ Your goals should always have a time frame and a value associated with them.

→ Prioritise your goals to establish which to start working towards first.

→ Divide your goals into emergency, lifestyle and retirement buckets, and fill your emergency bucket first.

Putting it into action

Now that you have identified exactly what you need to put aside to reach each of your goals, be sure to establish the appropriate savings accounts and start researching possible investments.

Rename the sub-accounts of any online high-interest savings accounts to something that reflects your savings goals (such as holiday or MBA).

You'll then need to set up the correct monthly transfers from your bills account to start building towards your goals.

CHAPTER 16
Protect
yourself

Bring a raincoat, definitely . . . or at least a little umbrella that can fit in your bag, because it always does rain.

Gwyneth Paltrow

We covered a lot of ground in the previous chapters, from unlearning our own bad habits to teaching our children great habits, from setting goals to achieving them, all the while learning tips to implement throughout our journey to wealth creation. There is still one more important area we need to cover before we are really ready to prosper, and that is protecting all this good work we are doing, so that nothing life can ever throw at us will defeat us financially.

We have set our goals, identified where we are now and started to build a plan to get us to where we need to be, and we can now appreciate that there is a gap, in financial terms, between the two. Provided we stick to our plan, we'll close that gap and ultimately reach our goal. However, there's always the possibility that life will throw us a curveball that prevents us from working and earning a living. It could be redundancy, illness, injury or even death.

Well, I hear you saying, if I'm dead it doesn't really matter, does it? And that may well be the case, provided there is no-one in your life who relies on you for money to help them meet their ongoing needs, such as a child or a partner, or even parents or other relatives. Until we have all the necessary financial resources to be fully self-sufficient, which for most of us isn't until retirement, we need to put a plan in place to protect us from the unexpected.

The problem of underinsurance

Just as we insure our car or home and contents against fire, theft and damage, we should insure ourselves. Underinsurance is a huge unresolved problem in Australia. A 2010 Rice Warner study estimated the overall level of underinsurance to meet the subsistence needs of families and dependants after death at $669 billion. The gap is even higher for injury or illness cover.

Suddenly finding oneself in the position of being unable to earn a living, but with plenty of bills still to pay, can cause serious financial strain. Creditors are rarely sympathetic at such times and will continue to beat the door down until their bills are paid, irrespective of the circumstances. A good personal insurance plan is a vital piece of the financial planning puzzle, because without it all our other plans could fall apart in an instant, and all our hard work would be for nothing.

Case study: Don't leave it until it's too late

A client of mine experienced just this scenario a couple of years ago. We'd just had our introductory meeting, during which we talked, among other things, about the fact that she had no insurance. She had never seen an adviser in the past and had never even considered that she needed insurance.

Claire was 36, had a high-paying professional job and was fairly good with her money. She had two properties at the time. Although she had managed to pay down almost 75 per cent of the mortgage on the house she lived in, she knew that every dollar had been going into her properties. She had not diversified into other investment areas and she had very little cash in the bank. All this was beginning to make her nervous, and as I talked her through our process she was clearly keen to start taking action. She was really excited about our first session, booked for the following week, when we would work through her actual life goals and personal values.

A few days later Claire was diagnosed with breast cancer. She had found a lump on Monday morning and went in for tests right away.

I was the first person she called when she found out. With no personal insurance, she knew she was in trouble financially.

Over the next six months, Claire underwent chemotherapy and radiation treatment. In the end she quit her job, as she felt that the stress of that position had potentially played a role in her becoming sick. Following the most intensive part of the treatment, Claire spent time reflecting on her life, as people in her situation frequently do, and when she started down her road to recovery she knew she wanted to make some big changes in her life.

After another few months Claire was in remission, and almost a year after her initial diagnosis she finally found work doing something she loved, a position that was far less demanding. It had taken her some time to settle on this role.

She had survived cancer and felt much happier in her new career, but Claire was severely disadvantaged financially during the 12 months she was not working. As she had built up some wealth through her two properties, she was ineligible for government support and was forced to sell the house she lived in and move into the smaller investment property in order to free up some cash to fund her living expenses and treatment costs. This financial burden, on top of the health crisis she was facing, added more stress than she could cope with at times. Selling the property was a huge step for her, and she was devastated that all her hard work was going down the drain when she could have been protected the whole time.

In some respects, Claire was one of the lucky ones as she did at least have some resources to fall back on, although she was then, at the age of 38, faced with the challenge of starting again financially. She still had quite a large mortgage on the investment property and very little cash in the bank, and was now earning a lower income in return for a job she felt more passionate about.

So what could Claire have done differently?

If Claire had had a comprehensive personal insurance plan in place when she got sick, it is likely she would have received a lump-sum payment of several hundred thousand dollars, as well as 75 per cent of her monthly salary for the duration of the period she was unable to work. This would of course have depended on what insurance she held. Let's now consider the options.

About personal insurance

There are four major types of personal insurance, all of which perform different functions, and in truth most of us need a little of each. Life insurance, trauma insurance, and total and permanent disability (TPD) insurance are all referred to as lump-sum cover. This means that in the event of a claim, a lump sum of money is paid to the policy owner. Income protection insurance is a monthly benefit that is paid out when someone is on claim and unable to work.

Let's now look at these insurances in more detail, as it is important to understand what each one covers, how and when it would be paid and in what situation you might need it. The next step is working out how much you need, because it is up to you to specify the amount of cover required when you apply. Of course, the higher the amount of cover you select, the more the premium will cost, so getting just enough is usually the preferred option.

Life insurance

This is the simplest type of insurance product to understand. Basically, if you die, the insurance company will pay out the sum insured to your nominated beneficiaries (or your estate). If you're alive, no dice! There's not really much ambiguity around being alive or being dead—hence the simplicity of this type of cover. That said, most life policies these days do build in a terminal illness benefit, which is an early release of the death benefit if you are diagnosed with a terminal illness and unlikely to live beyond 12 months.

What's it for?

Life insurance is best used to cover any debts you may have, so no-one else is left with the responsibility of paying them, and also to provide money that could be invested to furnish an income for someone who is financially dependent on you.

How much do I need?

A rule of thumb is to write down all your debts, then take away any assets that could be sold to reduce the debt. The difference between the two is probably an appropriate amount of life insurance cover. If you have financial dependants, you'll also need to work out how much income they would need on an annual basis, and for how many years they would need it.

Trauma insurance

Trauma insurance is my favourite personal insurance product. Some people call it living insurance, because it is essentially paid, not when you die, but when you are diagnosed with a critical illness. Most policies cover more than 50 serious medical conditions, the three most common being heart attack, cancer and stroke, although a myriad other conditions, such as multiple sclerosis, diabetes, severe burns or coma, are claimable. Each of the conditions covered has what's called a definition (these definitions vary slightly from policy to policy), which outlines the severity of the condition and what you actually need to be diagnosed with in order to be eligible for a claim. As mentioned, this is also a form of lump-sum cover that is paid to the insured upon diagnosis of a claimable condition.

What's it for?

The lump-sum payment you receive can be used for anything you like, really, but most importantly you will have the funds available to pay for potentially expensive medical treatment if required. You will face some serious choices in the event of a claim. The money could also be used to reduce debt, thereby reducing your stress, or to fund living expenses should you need or want to take time off work.

How much do I need?

I suggest applying for at least the equivalent of two years' worth of your current salary, or a minimum of $200 000. This level of cover would provide you with substantial flexibility, although you might also wish to include your current level of debt to fully protect yourself. This would mean you could repay all debt and take two years off work to recover in the event of a claim.

Total and permanent disability (TPD) insurance

TPD is probably the least claimed form of personal insurance cover, although it is still extremely important. Essentially it relates to your occupation, and a claim would be accepted if a medical diagnosis confirms that as a result of a disability you will never be able to work again. Commonly this would apply to someone who is paralysed or who loses a limb, but there are other claimable conditions such as severe mental illness.

What's it for?

Its main purpose is to cover loss of income. This is often a much larger sum of money than many of us might realise, especially if you are young and only just starting your wealth creation journey. The claim payout can also be used to provide for medical care and modifications in the home.

How much do I need?

If you have income protection insurance (as discussed next), some of the ongoing income burden would be relieved by these regular monthly payments, meaning you will need less TPD cover. Most importantly, you should aim to cover all your debts and then think about whether or not you can survive on 75 per cent of your current income (this is usually what you will receive in monthly payments from your income protection). If the answer is yes, then your current level of debts plus perhaps $100 000 to provide for medical treatment or home modifications might suffice. If you were to cover the full

100 per cent of your current income, you would need a much larger sum that could be invested to produce income for you to live on.

Income protection insurance

Income protection insurance does just that: it protects your monthly income in the event that you are unable to work for a period of time because of illness or injury. Provided a doctor has certified that you are unable to work (and you meet the policy terms and conditions), the income protection claim would be paid and you would receive a monthly payment until such time as you are healthy enough to return to work.

Waiting period

This refers to the length of time you select that you are willing to wait before being paid your monthly income protection benefits. The shorter the waiting period, the more expensive the premium. You can usually choose a period of 1, 14, 30, 60 or 90 days, or even up to two years. Bear in mind that you will need to dip into your savings during this period. Thirty days is a great starting point, but if you have managed to set aside three months' salary in a buffer account, you might consider extending your waiting period to 90 days and saving money on your premiums.

Benefit period

This refers to how long you will be paid the benefit. Ideally you should select a policy that will pay you to age 65, but you can also select two or five years. A policy that has an age 65 benefit period will continue to pay you a monthly benefit for as long as you are sick, right through to age 65 in a severe case, which would be comparable to TPD cover, as discussed earlier. If you select a two-year or five-year benefit period, the policy will pay you for those periods of time and then payments will cease even if you are still unable to return to work. These shorter benefit periods will reduce the cost of the insurance, but obviously a benefit period to age 65 will provide you with the most peace of mind.

What's it for?

This type of insurance is used to replace your regular source of income if you are ever unable to work because of illness or injury. The idea is that you can use the monthly benefits to cover your regular ongoing living expenses and commitments, which do not cease just because you are unable to work. This type of insurance is very important for young people starting out in the workforce, as they have so many years left to work and earn an income. It is also important for anyone who has a mortgage and/or family members relying on their income to survive.

How much do I need?

Insurance companies in Australia will insure up to 75 per cent of your current gross (before-tax) income and no more. This is usually a good starting point. If you are in the enviable situation that you have a lot of surplus funds each month after paying all expenses, you may find it appropriate to select a lower monthly benefit. This is not a common circumstance, however. Most people would find it very hard to live on less than their current full income, so 75 per cent is already going to stretch them.

There are slight variations in the conditions outlined above, depending on the insurer. Many insurance companies now offer income protection policies with a benefit period to age 70, recognising that we are now working longer than in the past. It's important to review all of your options with the help of a professional before you make any decisions.

Putting a quality plan in place

A qualified financial adviser can help you determine the exact level of insurance you need in all areas and run quotes across the entire marketplace to help you find the best value for your money. You will also find online calculators to help you, and as technology advances online services are emerging that permit you to calculate what you need, run quotes and even apply for a policy online. However, I recommend the services of a professional, as the application process can be lengthy and you won't always be accepted by the insurance company.

A professional adviser will also be able to review the underwriter's decision and advise you on whether or not it was fair. In some cases, the professional adviser may be able to work with you and the insurance company to negotiate some kind of compromise, resulting in your obtaining cover that you otherwise might not have been able to access. A good adviser will question you about your health history and will speak to some of the insurers to see which company is more likely to accept your case.

Because insurance companies are always trying to improve their product and service offerings, there are some situations where one company will accept an application that another company has turned down. This could be because the insurer hasn't had as many claims for a certain health condition, or because the company specialises in a particular type of occupation and is willing to accept a slightly higher level of risk in that area.

The insurance premiums charged to policy holders are based on a combination of national public statistics and each company's own internal claims history, so there are variations across time and between companies.

Remember, you are 'applying' for insurance

Despite what many may think, it is not your God-given right to be granted insurance. You are essentially applying to transfer the financial risk from yourself to the insurance company. The company must decide, with each and every application it receives, whether it is comfortable taking on that risk. This process is called underwriting, and involves the insurer's underwriters going through your application with a fine-tooth comb before arriving at a decision on whether or not you are a good prospect.

The insurance application is long and exhaustive, including questions about your age, sex, weight and height, and about your occupation, income and any risks associated with your work. It then goes through countless personal health questions, asking far more than you would imagine, and even covers personal habits and lifestyle questions.

If this seems excessive, you have to remember that once you are issued with a policy in Australia, and provided you keep paying your premiums, the insurer can *never* cancel the contract, so they need to satisfy themselves that you are not a high-risk case.

Insurance companies need to balance their books too, like any other business, carrying a good balance of risk, ensuring they are bringing in enough through premiums to be able to pay out the claims that arise. Obviously many policies will not be claimed on, so provided they are charging the right premiums and not taking on too many overly risky applicants, there should always be enough in the pool.

Those with a history of poor health will find it more difficult to obtain cover. That said, every type of pre-existing illness or injury is treated differently by the underwriters and carries with it a different risk rating. For example, asthma, which is something I suffer from, is not generally considered a huge claims risk. Any degenerative condition is likely to cause problems, however.

The most important thing is to complete the application fully and honestly. There's no point at all in skimming details or omitting information altogether. As soon as someone lodges a claim with the insurer, your Medicare record and entire medical history will be reviewed, and if the insurer finds that you purposely left something out of your application (this is referred to as non-disclosure), particularly if you have suffered an illness or injury they would never have accepted in the first place, there is a high probability they will not pay your claim.

That said, if you forgot to mention that you broke your arm as a child, or some other relatively minor condition or incident, it is unlikely this would affect your claim. This is common sense too. A bone broken when you were a child that has healed perfecly is not going to make you an insurance risk, whereas a degenerative disease such as diabetes certainly could.

Many people are sceptical about insurance companies, but when you think about it, the concept of insurance is incredibly powerful. In essence, if we pay just a little bit of our salary each year to hold a comprehensive insurance policy, we have bought peace of mind, knowing we will always have enough financial resources available.

Many Australians do not take seriously the responsibility to establish their own personal insurance plan, and sadly this results in a greater burden on society when tragedy strikes.

The Black Saturday tragedy

On 7 February 2009, when the devastating Black Saturday bushfires roared through the state of Victoria, some 173 people lost their lives and a further 414 were injured. The fires destroyed more than 2000 homes and 3500 other structures. This devastating event destroyed the lives and livelihoods of entire communities.

Unbelievably, only about $5 million was paid out in life insurance as a result of these fires, purely because most of the victims didn't have insurance in place. Perhaps they didn't know enough about insurance and how important it really was, or perhaps they felt they couldn't afford the premiums. This would have amounted to an average $29 000 per family who lost a loved one. In reality, the $5 million was paid out to about 15 per cent of victims, while the other 85 per cent had no insurance at all. In many cases, the person who lost their life was the breadwinner and main contributor to the financial security of the family.

After the tragedy, Australians banded together in an incredible fundraising effort to support the families of those who lost loved ones and those who lost their homes. But what if everyone had had adequate insurance? Potentially, the funds raised could have been used for higher level rehabilitation programs, counselling and support to rebuild communities, instead of barely being enough to cover many of the basic needs of those affected.

The community spirit shown during this horrible time was truly commendable, and I certainly don't wish to take anything away from that. But the events also illustrated in a particularly tragic way the potential consequences of underinsurance. I urge you to put an appropriate personal insurance plan in place to ensure you are doing the right thing by your loved ones and yourself.

In the previous pages I have recommended that you seek professional advice before putting a quality insurance plan in place. In the final chapter, I expand on the value financial advisers can add to your whole journey to financial security.

Key points

→ Almost everyone, unless they are wealthy, needs personal insurance.

→ Remember, you are 'applying' for insurance; it is not a right.

→ Obtain quality cover while you are young and healthy.

→ It could happen to you; insurance gives you peace of mind.

Putting it into action

Review your personal insurance needs and check that you have the appropriate levels of cover in place. You may have insurances within your superannuation fund that you don't know about, so check your most recent paper statement, log in online or call your superannuation provider to check what cover you have.

If you are unsure about how to go about this, enlist the services of a professional insurance adviser or financial adviser, because it is really the most important part of your financial plan.

CHAPTER 17

Seek and
share
advice

Whatever we possess becomes of double value when we have the
opportunity of sharing it with others.

Jean-Nicolas Bouilly

As noted in the previous chapter, the help of a professional when putting together your insurance plan can mean the difference between getting your policy accepted and having no cover at all. I'm a big advocate of using professional advisers in all areas of your life, and not just because I am myself a financial adviser! There a couple of reasons I think it is important.

A lot goes into managing your personal finances. I know, because my team spend countless hours every month, on every client, ensuring all is going to plan. There are many administration tasks involved, including setting up and managing different accounts, keeping track of what's going on and updating records when required, not to mention liaising with all the different organisations involved, such as banks, insurance companies, fund managers and billers. Even simple tasks such as paying an account or notifying of a change of address can be time-consuming when you have to wait in a telephone queue each time.

What is your time worth?

Many of us don't stop to think about what our time is actually worth, in other words to think of our time as a type of currency. As we apply the principle of value for money in other areas, it is important we also demand value for our time spent.

I employ a house cleaner for this very reason. I have calculated the value of my time and made a decision to hire someone instead of spending my own time on cleaning. First, my time is worth substantially more than the rate my cleaner charges me, and second, I absolutely hate cleaning! With the busy lifestyle I have, my weekends are precious and I'm far happier spending them with my partner and my friends, or even working on my business, than I would be cleaning the bathroom. I'm not saying this works for everyone—my sister, for one, actually loves cleaning—but it's important to think about what your time is worth and how you want to spend it.

Saving money by doing something yourself poorly will likely only cost you in the long run. In my case, I would probably actually *never* clean my house—it wouldn't even be a matter of my doing a bad job; I just wouldn't do it at all. Then I would argue with Finn about it, because he doesn't really like cleaning either, and the situation would put unnecessary pressure on our relationship. I'd end up sad, single and living in a dirty house—a risk I'm just not willing to take!

Exercise: Establish your worth

The first step in working out how much your time is worth is simply to take your annual salary, divide it by 48 weeks, and then divide that number by 40 hours (or roughly the number of hours you work). For example, someone on a salary of $85 000 has an hourly rate of $44.27.

Table 17.1 provides you with a quick-and-dirty way to calculate your hourly rate, based on your annual salary on the left and the hours you work each week along the top.

Table 17.1: calculating your hourly rate

Salary/Hours	25	30	35	40	45	50	60
$30 000	$25	$21	$18	$16	$14	$13	$10
$40 000	$33	$28	$24	$21	$19	$17	$14
$50 000	$42	$35	$30	$26	$23	$21	$17
$60 000	$50	$42	$36	$31	$28	$25	$21
$70 000	$58	$49	$42	$36	$32	$29	$24
$80 000	$67	$56	$48	$42	$37	$33	$28
$100 000	$83	$69	$60	$52	$46	$42	$35
$120 000	$100	$83	$71	$63	$56	$50	$42
$140 000	$117	$97	$83	$73	$65	$58	$49
$150 000	$125	$104	$89	$78	$69	$63	$52
$200 000	$167	$139	$119	$104	$93	$83	$69
$250 000	$208	$174	$149	$130	$116	$104	$87
$300 000	$250	$208	$179	$156	$139	$125	$104

Once you know what you earn for every hour you work, you can start to make smarter decisions about how you should be spending your time. And knowing how many hours it has taken you to earn your money helps you make good decisions when spending it. If you earn $50 000 a year and work 35 hours per week, your hourly rate is approximately $30. Next time you pick up the $90 dinner bill for you and your 'friend' who never seems to repay the favour, you might weigh up the fact that you had to work for 1.5 hours to pay for her meal. In future you might opt to spend that on a fortnightly cleaner instead!

Experts add value

My cleaner is probably a better cleaner than I am and most certainly more efficient, because he is experienced and he does it all day long. He knows the best products to use, how to reach all the difficult corners, the fastest way to dust, and which is the best head on the vacuum cleaner for the different carpets and floor surfaces. He's good at it, so I let him do it. As a result, my house is always clean and fresh and lovely.

Using the help of a professional or expert should certainly add value to your situation, because they will undoubtedly know more about it than you do. Not only will they likely have formal qualifications in their area of specialty, but they will be far more efficient than you could hope to be because they do what they do all day, every day. They'll know all of the details that you might overlook, and will be able to make decisions and recommendations based on the years of experience they have built up. They will ensure you don't miss anything important and help you avoid making poor decisions based on a lack of deep understanding.

Keeping you accountable

Probably the most important role of any professional adviser is to keep you informed and accountable. My lawyer emails me every year to ask me if my will or powers of attorney need to be updated, and she lets me know whenever changes in legislation might affect me. With everything else I have on my plate already, I couldn't possibly stay on top of that. Meanwhile I'm busy doing the same thing in the area of finance for my clients, as you will be in your line of work.

A financial adviser will act as your personal financial coach, encouraging you as you reach milestones and keeping you motivated when times get tough. Your adviser will help you adjust your plan as circumstances change, because we know life always throws up challenges along the way, usually right when things are going well. Simply knowing that someone else is looking over your finances, and that you'll have to answer to them at your regular meeting, will keep you accountable and help you stick to your plan.

You might be able to get there on your own, but for most of us selecting the right adviser to have by our side throughout our journey will prove to be the smartest decision we'll ever make.

Selecting an adviser

When searching for a professional in any situation, it's most important to find not only someone who is experienced and qualified to do the job you're asking of them, but also someone whom you like and trust. In choosing a good financial adviser, consider the following:

- Have they asked you about your goals and what is important to you?

- Are they qualified and experienced? They should hold at a minimum a Diploma in Financial Services (Financial Planning); have provided you with a *Financial Services Guide*; and be an authorised representative either of their own Australian Financial Services Licence (AFSL) or of a larger company that holds an AFSL.

- Are they a member of a professional association, such as the Association of Financial Advisers?

- Do you like them?

- Do you trust them?

In all honesty, the last two questions are probably the most important. Of course they must have the relevant experience and qualifications, but if you don't feel comfortable with them and have a good feeling when you finish a meeting, you probably should keep looking. The idea of working with a financial adviser is that you can develop a long-term, supportive relationship, and if you want real results you'll need to be completely honest, open and comfortable with them.

Involve your friends—open up

In my opinion, one of the biggest barriers we face to getting ahead with our finances is that the topic of money is considered taboo in most circles. We generally don't share our financial situation even with our friends or family, apart from making a few flippant comments about spending too much on something or about what a bargain we may have found. And such conversation is always very superficial, never delving into detail, and therefore not very transparent or useful.

There can be a bit of a stigma attached to someone who is perceived not to be doing well financially. On the flipside, for those who do get their financial house in order, perhaps starting to earn a better salary and generally thriving financially, this success too is generally not discussed, for fear of appearing arrogant. It's a no-win situation that tends to draw a cloak of silence over the subject of money in polite conversation.

It all seems a little old-fashioned to me. If we actually started sharing our financial situation with selected friends and family, many benefits could result.

As with anything in life, you have a choice as to who you share this information with and precisely what you share, so always be sensible. Still, if you really want to start getting your financial situation in order, why not share your goals with close friends or family and seek their support? If those around you understand what you are trying to achieve and that you have a plan in place to get there, it is likely they will encourage you, motivate you and become a part of that journey. You may even find that you have a positive influence on them, and that they are encouraged to make fruitful changes to their situation too.

Many of my clients are referred by family members, or good friends, who are existing clients, and there really is a difference in their attitudes to money going forward. Because we get down to the basics, and resolve the fact that money simply facilitates the type of life we want to live, their ability to share their dreams with each other grows. It's amazing to witness two clients together openly sharing their aims and goals and how they are determined to stick to the plan. The support they can offer each other is phenomenal.

Share your wealth creation journey

I'm a keen runner, but I'm absolutely terrible at motivating myself if I'm on my own. Over the years I have built up an amazing circle of friends who all love to run, and each morning at 6 am we meet at the Tan in Melbourne for a workout. The first benefit of this is that as I have others to meet, when my alarm goes at 5.30 am I'm straight up and out the door because I don't want to let them down.

The second benefit is that we share our health and fitness goals with one another, including what we are training for and how we're going to get there. Being around fellow enthusiasts simply breeds focus and motivation. Over the years we have run countless half-marathons together, and ultra-marathons, and we've all embarked on full marathon journeys and supported one another in doing so. This may mean simple things like teeing up three of us to do an individual hour run, back to back, with whoever is training for a marathon, so they don't face their three-hour training run on their own. We've shared health-food kicks, organic retreats and yoga weekends away. I've shared so, so many amazing health and fitness experiences with these people over the years, and the bonus is that I have always remained fit.

Health and fitness are such a big part of my life now, because I have these amazing women to share the journey with. We don't give up on each other, we don't let each other down, we share the accomplishments and the injuries and setbacks, but we keep going. Because next year is another year, and I know that every morning at six someone will be waiting for me at the Tan.

I've done the same thing in business. Because I want to build successful, dynamic and growing businesses, I know I can't do it alone. I surround myself with other business owners and entrepreneurs and I share my successes, failures and challenges with them. This way I can learn from them, take action and constantly improve my businesses.

Sitting alone in my office trying to build the perfect company with no input from anyone would get me nowhere fast. I'd have to learn from all of my own mistakes, and it would take a lot longer to get results. It would also mean that I wasn't helping anyone else. Because when you share, you often have no idea how much the person you share with needs to hear what you have to offer. Imagine if someone has a similar financial goal to you, but they are really struggling to make it work. By sharing experiences you will likely be able to help each other and most certainly you will each feel less alone. Together you'll be able to motivate and encourage each other.

So pick the most supportive, motivated and encouraging people you know with whom to share your wealth creation journey. Hopefully they are already, or soon will be, on their own amazing journey, and together you will achieve great things. A little competitive spirit is great too. There's absolutely nothing wrong with being motivated to save a little faster because your friend is kicking some serious goals. I know I run harder when I'm getting beaten up the hill, and that's not a bad thing at all. It makes me fitter and stronger.

Key points

→ Know what your time is worth.

→ Experts can add value in areas you may not have thought of.

→ Pick advisers who are qualified and experienced, but whom you also like and trust.

→ Share your journey with supportive, motivated and encouraging people.

Putting it into action

Start your own slow money group! Pick a group of like-minded friends who you would be comfortable sharing your financial situation with and suggest a monthly (or even weekly) catch up where you get together and discuss each of your financial goals and how you are tracking towards them.

Select people who are also willing to share so that you can all work together to help each other. This might seem challenging, or even silly, however just remind yourself and those you've asked that the most successful men and women in the world often have mastermind groups of some kind, with different focuses in order to support their success in another way.

Setting goals, creating vision boards, finding ways to stay on track and accountable, as well as celebrating success are all proven strategies that lead to positive outcomes.

Just
do
it!

A journey of a thousand miles begins with a single step.

Lao Tzu

In this book I have argued that we should allow no special circumstances, no unlucky breaks, to stop us from achieving our aims in life. By identifying where we are now, setting our goals, building a plan and backing it all up with a good insurance plan ... well, it's already in the bag really.

The main reason we don't achieve what we set out to is simply that we don't follow through by taking the necessary action. We think about making big changes, we dream of acting differently, but then we just keep on going about things in the way we always have.

I love Albert Einstein's definition of insanity: 'doing the same thing over and over again and expecting different results'. We could apply this insight to many different aspects of our lives but especially, I believe, to our personal financial management. Let's face it, it's not easy to introduce momentous change into our lives, yet we are all most certainly capable of doing so. It's simply a matter of *taking action*.

By starting small, but starting now, we can all build sustainable wealth and get rich slow, whatever 'rich' may mean to us. It's about pushing forward, little by little, towards our goals, persistently sticking to the plan and staying focused, because it will work . . .

Good luck on your journey! I wish you all the health, wealth and happiness you deserve.

Index

Wealth Enhancers

Wealth Enhancers is a financial advisory firm with a difference. It's a place where dreaming is mandatory, planning is our culture, growing is a daily occurrence, and achievement is normal. If you're a motivated and enthusiastic person, we'd love to meet you.

Visit us at **www.wealthenhancers.com.au**, introduce yourself and start your own journey towards financial freedom.

You can also contact us here:
Twitter: @WealthEnhancers
Facebook: facebook.com/wealthenhancers
Vimeo: vimeo.com/channels/wealthenhancerstv

LEAGUE of extraordinary women.

League of Extraordinary Women

As young women with companies of our own, we struggled to find events where like-minded young female business owners could come together to share, support, encourage and inspire each other. My co-founder Sheryl Thai and I resorted to organising small monthly events of our own to fill this gap. Now, together with Liz Atkinson, Marie Cruz and the enthusiasm of a 'league' of extraordinary women, we have created the most exciting and largest group of young female entrepreneurs in Australia. Join us today at **www.leagueofextraordinarywomen.com.au**.

You can also contact the League here:
Twitter: @TheLeagueAust
Facebook: facebook.com/leagueofextraordinarywomen

Wrightbooks

Learn more with practical advice from our experts

How to Retire in 12 Months
Serena Star-Leonard

Money for Nothing
Justine Davies

Money Makeover
moneygirl.com.au

Shopping for Shares, 2E
Tracey Edwards

Financial Planning DIY Guide
Sam Henderson

Paper Flow
MaryAnne Bennie & Brigitte Hinneberg

Living Thin
Antonia Magee

The Property Diaries
Antonia Magee

The Great Life Redesign
Caroline Cameron

Available in print and e-book formats